Living
The Life You Want

Your personal key to true abundance
and the richness of everyday experience

Sylvia Clare and David Hughes

D1337754

PATHWAYS

First published in 2000 by
How To Books Ltd, 3 Newtec Place,
Magdalen Road, Oxford OX4 1RE, United Kingdom
Tel: 01865 793806 Fax: 01865 248780

British Library Cataloguing in Publication Data
A catalogue record for this book is available from
the British Library

Edited by Diana Brueton   Cover image PhotoDisc
Cover design by Shireen Nathoo Design

Produced for How To Books by Deer Park Productions
Typeset by PDQ Typesetting, Stoke-on-Trent, Staffs.
Printed and bound in Great Britain

Note: The material contained in this book is set out in good
faith for general guidance and no liability can be accepted for
loss or expense incurred as a result of relying in particular
circumstances on statements made in the book. The laws and
regulations are complex and liable to change, and readers
should check the current position with the relevant
authorities before making personal arrangements.

Pathways is an imprint of
How To Books

Contents

List of Illustrations

Preface

Living the life you want: what does this mean to you? Is it possible? Is it available to some people but not others? What are the differences between those who do and those who do not live the life they actually want to live?

We would argue that you can have exactly what you want in life *if* you also believe in that. Your beliefs play the biggest part in creating your reality. Most of us are taught to think much more in terms of limitation and low self-worth than we realise until we start to ask questions. Do we deserve a better life? Or do we get the life we deserve because that is what we believe we are entitled to? That is, we get what we envisage life holds for us.

Can positive thinking really make all the difference? Do what you think and believe really affect the daily realities of life? Most of the spiritual psychologies say all of this, and more, is possible if you learn to explore your own consciousness and see what is really lying there.

For my parents' generation, to seek psychological analysis was to admit that 'you had something wrong with you'. To be introspective was to be selfish and self-indulgent. The middle-aged hippy generation of today grew up believing that all you needed was love. The trouble was they thought love meant specific types of behaviour, free sexual expression, breaking down old systems, old attitudes and old beliefs. That was throwing the baby out with the bath water. No generation gets it all wrong and none so far in history has got it all right.

Recent changes in thinking show more and more people recognising they do have real choices in life. We can now choose many different lifestyles in western society without being deemed deviant. We have the notion of consumer choice and have had our eyes opened to the psychological tricks used in marketing. We have seen more people seeking a spiritual identity away from the traditional religious structures. We have recognised that war and aggression achieve little and now talk in terms of keeping the peace. The whole thinking of our society is slowly turning.

Society is made up of people – you and me – so if we change our own inner structures, the social structure in which we live will also change. Many have called this the new age of enlightenment, but as many traditions teach – 'before enlightenment, wash dishes and sweep floors, after enlightenment, wash dishes and sweep floors'. The difference is in the feelings we have towards what we do in life, how we do it and if we are doing what is right for us.

If society is made up of us all, everything we do affects everyone else equally. Everything is interrelated. It's rather like when are at school and the whole class is put into detention because one classmate will not own up to hiding the board rubber from the teacher. One person does not have the courage to admit they made a mistake and accept responsibility for their own behaviour so the rest of us suffer. Unless, that is, we all start telling the truth. No one wants to be the first to tell our mates they need to change. We have no right to, either. But we can change our selves and act as examples of how change brings benefits beyond comparison into our lives.

It is up to each and every one of us to stop blaming the people around us for our limitations in life and to start creating the life we really want to live. It might not be easy, it might take some time, but anything really worth having is worth putting some effort into, and that starts with recognising that your life is worth it too. This book cannot tell you everything or do it for you, but it does provide most of the directions and perspectives that will enable you to make real changes in your own life – because we are all worth it.

Sylvia Clare and David Hughes

Introduction:
What is Living Abundantly

Your birthright is to experience an abundance of love and harmony, both emotional and material. If we are honest that is the life we all want to lead. Abundance is limitless. It is the manifestation of energy in all possible forms. But we are taught in varying degrees, not to see or understand this concept and find it hard to imagine that this can possibly be true.

Living abundantly is an active process, nothing comes from nothing and everything comes from carefully directed effort. In its purest form living abundantly is simply love but this can express itself in many different ways, including the beauty of a summer sky or a full plate of food shared with friends. It can also mean your employment being completely fulfilling and an act of joy.

Perception and reality

Most people have an abundance deficit in one or more areas of their lives. This means they do not feel their needs are being met. We all have different perceptions of what we expect for ourself.

But for many, it is the perception that our needs are not met, the feeling that something is missing, that we could get more satisfaction out of life if we could only do/have the next thing on our list. More often than not, it is a fear that our needs may not be met tomorrow, or next week or next year.

Perceptual change and real change

So living abundantly is an active approach to life that requires effort from you. Effort in the form of being willing to effect change, in the following ways:

♦ By adapting your perceptual framework on life.
♦ By not worrying about the next day or week or year.

♦ By being able to make plans and trust that however they work out will be for your highest possible good.

♦ By being able to see the cup as half full and not half empty.

This book is about creating change in the fullest sense of the word, both perceptual and practical. It provides opportunities to examine your beliefs and create change for yourself.

Lack mentality

The opposite of living abundantly is living with a lack mentality and believing in limitation – that there is not enough to go round, that if someone has something then I am missing out. This is our cultural norm. Many of us are programmed with this perception and interpretation of life.

If we all choose a more abundant life of love and respect, we create a society that benefits from a position of total freedom, not from fear of punishment, reprisal and social exclusion. If we accept that everything we think, say or do represents a choice at conscious or unconscious level, we can choose a life that is really the life we want to live.

What it all really means

Living the abundant life means feeling confident and secure.

♦ It means living spontaneously, for the moment, but with responses that allow you to be confident your future will be taken care of.

♦ It means putting your confidence and reliance in yourself and not in something or someone that may let you down.

♦ It means understanding the relationship between your thoughts and your reality.

♦ It means finding your own set of principles to live by.

This book looks at teaching from NLP, humanistic psychology, Buddhism, Christianity and metaphysics. Without asking you to 'become' anything, except more of your whole self, it leads you through ideas and approaches that will enable you to lead a more abundant life.

Getting what you want in life means getting your mind working for, not against, you.

Knowing What You Want

W hat is the point of our life? This question occurs to most of us from time to time. The simple answer is that there is a very significant point to it all but sometimes we spend too much time asking the question instead of living the answer. The answer lies within our reach once we know where to look for it. This book will help you explore your own experiences and find your own answers to this and other questions.

The common experience

Life moves at an increasingly fast pace. We are taught to measure ourselves by the models of success offered by society. We are driven by desires to have, or to be other than we are. Many of us feel dissatisfied with our lives, at some level, no matter what we achieve. Eventually the new car or next holiday ceases to pacify those feelings.

Levels of relationship breakdown, stress, depression and related physical illness are increasing at alarming rates, in spite of us all seeming to have so much. This leads to a general state of confusion about the missing component, and whose responsibility it is to fix it for us. We are left with a sense that things are not as we would wish them to be. We tend to accept that the best thing is to put up with what we have – but does this leave us truly contented? It often means we are missing out on huge areas of our own potential.

> If you keep doing what you've always done, you'll keep getting what you've always got.

This book offers powerful tools for transformation and provides personally challenging choices for everyone. To achieve our heart's desire in life we must first ask questions of ourselves, starting with:

- ◆ What do you really want?
- ◆ How much do you feel in control of your life?
- ◆ How much choice do you feel you have in life?
- ◆ What are you really capable of?
- ◆ What is the truth about the real you – your hidden potential?
- ◆ How can you transform your life?

Knowing your own mind

Your mind is the most powerful tool you have. It is the tool with which you can change your whole life if you choose to do so. Like any tool, it is how you use it that counts.

> You can use your mind for improving your life, or you can ignore its potential and allow your mind, and life, to continue as they are.

Your mind is the basis of all your potential, so exploring its content is one aspect this book considers in depth. But it is also in the potential of your imagination that the future lies. By distinguishing the differences between various aspects of the mind we can recognise and transform our mind processes. There are real opportunities to change your life by following a series of simple yet profoundly effective stages that lead you to a fuller understanding of self. Each step is to be taken in your own time and space. For this reason, it is a good idea to keep a written record of your responses to the exercises. This helps you recognise your beliefs and desires at deeper levels, as you read further through the book.

Try it now

Decide if any of the following statements apply to your life.
- ◆ Whenever I get what I think I want, there always seems to be something missing.
- ◆ Things never work out the way they ought to.
- ◆ I always feel that I have to accept what life offers me, it's not in my control.
- ◆ I often feel guilty if I get what I want.
- ◆ If I get what I think I want I usually find it is not what I wanted.
- ◆ Even when I know what I want there's always some reason why I can't have or keep it.

How do these statements make you feel? The more time you spend considering your present position the more you will achieve from the exercises that follow. Note how you respond to these statements now, and come back a week later to see if your responses are the same. You might be surprised at how much your thoughts and feelings can change over time.

Recognising your present position

It is surprisingly common for people to have these feelings, in spite of a nagging voice in the back of our minds saying 'it doesn't need to be like this'. Many people have stopped questioning these experiences and instead question themselves, assuming that they are the inadequate ones, not the thought structures they live within. It is this assumption that keeps us trapped in a treadmill of desire and disappointment. There are three key aspects to this first section:

♦ Knowing what you really want in life.
♦ Gently and assertively going for it and not being diverted.
♦ Living your life in a state of balanced calm and trust and getting the most out of each experience.

In order to achieve this you will need to:

♦ Examine, appreciate and respect all you have in your life.
♦ Learn to recognise the difference between what you *really* want and what you *think* you want.
♦ Succeed in achieving all you want, whilst remaining compassionate and caring towards other people.
♦ Learn to relax, stay calm and trust that your heart's desire will come to you, if you let it.

Developing creative skills

You will be taken through several steps, each offering examples that illustrate a stage in the process, until you fully understand your own heart's desires and the process becomes automatic. This will also positively affect all those who are close to you, and who work and live around you.

A desire, an intention, a wish or an affirmation is like a prayer:

◆ It can only be answered if you trust that it will.

◆ It cannot be answered if you hold a negative belief, ie wishes don't come true or only for some people.

Any contradictions in our deeply held beliefs will override our desires and wishes. So wishes can come true for those who believe in them. It is often said in stories that only people who believe in fairies can see them. Life is rather like that too, and we hope you will come to understand the profound truth of this as you read further.

Recognising intentions

What is an intention? It is the conscious or unconscious motivation behind any act or behaviour. Whether we are aware of it or not, everything we do has a motive or purpose. So what are your intentions in life? We are often quite unaware of why we behave in certain ways. Becoming more aware of your purpose or agenda will lead to you a greater sense of what true abundance really means.

Your intentions are important. They are a clear expression of how you value yourself and how you demonstrate that to others.

1 A vague intention suggests you have no real intention at all, and therefore do not believe there is anything better for you in this life.

2 A half-hearted intention suggests you do not really consider yourself worth putting much effort into.

3 A fully committed intention suggests you consider yourself a worthwhile investment.

Try it now   Write down any intentions you are aware of. What do you hope to get out of life? Spend some time thinking about this. What aspect of yourself or your life would you like to:

◆ know

◆ understand

◆ develop

◆ change?

Make notes on any thoughts and feelings that come up. Don't dismiss anything. Whatever you think and feel is a part of your consciousness and therefore important to the process. No one has comfortable thoughts and feelings all the time but denying them does not take them away. They will influence your success. Note examples from your own real experiences as well.

Do your answers include any of these responses?

◆ Even when I know what I want no one else takes any notice.

◆ It doesn't seem to matter how hard I try, something or someone else always needs to come first.

◆ People/life seem to take advantage of me so easily.

◆ What I want always gets overlooked or ignored by others around me.

◆ I always end up getting upset or frustrated by other people.

Most of the scenarios in the section above occur because we are not assertive enough about giving our needs equal priority to those of others. This is because we do not value ourselves enough. And if we do not think we are worth it, then why should anyone else?

> Quietly hoping someone else will fulfil your needs and dreams is not the best way to get what you want in your life. You have to do it for yourself.first.

Recognising your need for assertiveness

Assertiveness is not about getting our own way. Being assertive is:

(a) being able to state your feelings and get what you want out of life without being controlling, or controlled by others, or by situations.

(b) releasing fear and allowing yourself to be your true self.

(c) being able to respond responsibly 'response-ability' rather than reacting.

(d) about living in harmony with everything and everyone and allowing each individual to be themselves in their own way.

(e) about taking responsibility for yourself and openly accepting your own fallibility.

Knowing your whole self

This means being your whole self, not just a cut down version
that:

◆ feels easy
◆ conforms to what you think you ought to be
◆ conforms to what others want you to be.

None of your attributes are wrong or undesirable, they just
haven't been mastered and put to their best possible use. We
all spend too much of our lives in denial of who we really are.

> *The Snow Goose need not bathe itself to make itself white.*
> *Neither need you do anything but be yourself.* LaoTzu

To achieve this we first have to know ourselves very well. With
that knowledge, we gain a quiet strength. This enables us to
respond freely to everything that occurs around us without
seeking to change others. Once we know who we are and what
we want, it becomes much easier to be gently assertive in our
lives and live the life we choose. To really live and let live.

Dealing with difficulty

If something happens that we do not like, we can choose how
to deal with it:

1 We can become angry or fearful. This might be what the
   person who provoked that intended, so we are allowing
   ourselves to be controlled and manipulated. We are not
   being true to ourselves.

2 We can choose to become angry as an expression of our
   right to express our feelings, our disagreement. This might
   create fear in another party and cause further division.

3 We might choose to side-step the issues and carry on doing
   our own thing, a passive response. This might be avoidance
   rather than skilful communication.

4 We might choose to confront the issue calmly and refuse to
   be manipulated into an emotion to please another, but also
   refuse to be silenced. This response respects the rights of all
   parties and seeks true resolution.

You may be able to think of some additional choices of response you have made in your own life. Make a note of these in your workbook. Each response says something about you, how you feel about yourself, your self-respect and self-value. Consider each of these examples and decide which ones are most like you.

The word responsible means able to respond:

◆ the ability to choose your response
◆ to understand the implications of your choice
◆ to accept responsibility for the outcome of your choice.

Becoming assertive

Most assertiveness training emphasises working on how to deal with a situation, and learning new styles of communication. But in my experience lack of assertiveness usually means that:

◆ we do not know what we really want
◆ we do not really believe that we deserve it
◆ we do not really believe that we are entitled to ask for it
◆ we fear the reaction of others to our self-expression
◆ we expect disappointment.

These result in slow build-ups of frustration and anger. These emotions have the potential to damage us if we hold on to them.

There is a different approach which will show you:

1 How to decide what you want and how to invite that into your life, quietly and confidently.

2 How to assess the difference between what you really want and what you think you want.

3 How to relax and trust that whatever you most wish for will come.

4 How to approach your life in a more open way that creates less stress.

Relaxing into the process

If our brain, or mind, is relaxed we are more likely to achieve what we want. If our mind is filled with conflicting information and beliefs, we are going to have conflicting experiences in our lives. This can only muddy our dreams and intentions, and lead to disappointment. One of the most important things to remember is the self-fulfilling prophesy: your thoughts create your reality, totally and utterly. So clarity and consistency of beliefs, together with a relaxed approach to life, is the only way to make sure you are getting what you really want.

> Remember, *all your thoughts create all your reality.* There is no exception to this principle.

Learning to visualise

Many techniques in psychology and healing use visualisation to achieve change in people's lives. This is commonly done by:

♦ **future pacing** – bringing the future to the present, as if it is reality now

♦ **seeing** where we want to be at a certain point in the future and 'seeing' the stages leading there.

> Nothing exists in human experience that did not once begin as a creative thought in someone's imagination.

Both techniques use the visual imagination capacities of our right brain, which is also where most of the unconscious activity appears to come from. It is the deeply held beliefs from our unconscious mind that can block us in achieving our desired reality. Visualisation methods help to counteract those deeply held blocks by exposing them. Once exposed, we have the choice of releasing them so that we can move on. Some people find these techniques easier than others, but persevere and work with them.

Try it now   Sit still and close your eyes. Now visualise something you are very familiar with, eg your bedroom/living room/car/favourite clothes, etc. Describe it to someone else in detail. How did you know what to describe?

There are three types of creative visualisation:

1 Creating a visual image of something which you already know, as it exists in memory.

2   Creating a visual image using a guided visualisation technique, eg tape, workshop, guides.

4   Creating visual imagery that is original to you.

These can be combined to create endless possibilities.

Often when we say 'see' we mean 'sense' too. Some people just 'know things' but do not see them in a visual way. The format is not important, it is the outcome that matters.

Creating with memories

Memory is creative in endless ways. Research shows that our memories are rarely accurate because everything is expressed in terms of our own perceptual framework. Memories are only ever a version of events which we choose to perceive, so we are already being creative with what 'exists'. Thus it is quite possible to review memories and to take a different perspective, one which changes the memory as a form of self-healing and letting go.

Try it now

The following visualisation will help you to relax, and also to begin to use your imagination to create images and work them through in your mind. It is a good idea to read this onto a tape for yourself, and use it to clear your mind and focus your thoughts.

Make sure you are warm, comfortable, sitting upright and will not be disturbed for the duration. You can decide how long you want to stay in this visualisation. Close your eyes and take a couple of minutes to focus on your breathing. Notice each in and each out breath. With each out breath allow yourself to relax a little more deeply, to let go of your tension as you let go of your breath. When you know you are relaxed enough to work, turn on your tape with this script.

The peaceful valley
Imagine you are standing on a hill, looking down into a beautiful valley. The valley is lush and green, full of trees and flowers. You can feel yourself wanting to reach this lovely, peaceful place. You can sense its tranquillity and beauty, its natural calm and acceptance of all that moves and grows in it. You know that it will accept you in the same way, that whatever or whoever you are, the valley will

welcome and embrace you in its calm, soothing atmosphere.

The slope in front of you is gentle. As you begin to walk down it, with each step allow yourself to release your mind and body more and more deeply. The steps you take are leading you down into this lovely place, a place where you can really relax and let go, a place where you can just be. You can hear the birds singing joyfully in their freedom. A gentle breeze keeps you cool in the sunshine, rippling across the grass in waves of perfumed colour and delicate texture. As you now reach the flat ground you look for somewhere you can rest, either sitting or lying, just staying in this valley as long as you want to, letting go and being in a state of pure existence. Stay in your valley for as long as you want to, getting to know it, so that you can return here whenever you want just by shutting your eyes.

When you are ready to leave this place gently open your eyes and bring yourself back to the present.

Using a visualisation like this is one of the most effective forms of being internally relaxed and creative. It is a way of clearing away negative thoughts and feelings which will block our sense of abundance.

> Practising any form of deep relaxation daily is one of the most important techniques and accomplishments for being able to create a life that is all you want it to be.

Following your body's natural rhythms

Within your body are several natural rhythms that affect your experiences. One of the most influential is the **ultradian rhythm**. This is the natural cycle of brain activity levels that continue throughout the day and night on a roughly 90-minute basis. It regulates our dreaming patterns and which side of the brain is functioning at any given time. The dreamy times are when our right cerebral cortex is functioning most effectively. This is where our imagination, creativity and intuitive functions operate from and they are most effectively accessed when we are dreamy or drowsy.

Taking brain breaks

This is an opportunity to experience additional techniques which you can incorporate into your daily life.

◆ Do you find that at a certain time of the day you really cannot concentrate and function properly, your thinking is muzzy and all you want to do is to go off into a daydream?
◆ Note the time of day when this normally occurs.
◆ How often do you feel this slump? Is it once or twice a day?
◆ Do you allow yourself to go with the feeling in the moment?
◆ Do you fight it or struggle with it and feel frustrated that you can't get your brain to 'work properly'?

This is what we call your 'slump' time. Your brain is actually working very well but it is the part of your brain that does not like to think logically or 'work' in conventionally accepted terms. It is the part of your brain that wants to play and create. This is one of the most versatile states for relaxing and making the most of your creativity. It wants to daydream, something that we are conditioned to believe is a waste of time. But if you can make this into a routine you will find it very beneficial.

Try it now   Make sure you have at least 15–20 minutes for this exercise and will not be disturbed. If you do this at work, arrange to take a short break. It will make you more effective later on. Take a deep breath and allow yourself to drift away. Make a conscious note to allow yourself to come back to full awareness within your allocated time. Trust you will do this. If you are uncertain, set a small alarm to bring you back. Do not attempt to time it consciously in your thoughts or you will be working against this mind state. It is 'letting go'.

Daydreaming

Daydreaming is letting your mind wander freely. We also call this **drift dreaming** because it is letting your mind drift and wander where it chooses, not where you choose. This allows you to observe your thoughts from an external position. If you find yourself concentrating on a certain problem or issue, just tell your thoughts that you will return to it when you are in a different frame of mind. This develops essential skills in thought awareness and management. It is essential to be able to monitor your thought patterns and to emotionally detach from them at will. You then achieve greater levels of self-mastery and increase your ability to find true abundance.

To follow these techniques, choose a time which is your normal slump time and allow yourself to go into a natural trance. After lunch is often a good time. Agree with yourself a time to allow yourself to 'slump and see what happens'.

When you have practised this, start to add creative visualisations to it – use one of the visualisations from this book, or create your own. Use tapes if you find it easier to have a voice guiding you.

Summary

Your life is your own greatest work of creation and you can change whatever you do not like, you can rework the canvas any time.

- ◆ Take time to get to know your self more fully and you will find, without exception, that you are worth it.
- ◆ Make a commitment to yourself to value yourself and to spend time developing the skills of self-knowledge.
- ◆ Recognise that there may be a difference between what you think you want and what you really want.
- ◆ Acknowledge that changes to, and recognition of, your needs, wishes and dreams can only come from you.
- ◆ Relaxing into the process of change and development creates a better basis for all self-mastery work.
- ◆ Using the mind creatively, such as through visualisation, is a skill which everyone can develop.

CHAPTER 2

Learning How to Create

G enerally Western society attaches little value to imagination. We are told 'it's just your imagination, it's not real'. If we daydreamed at school, we were told not to waste time. Thus:

♦ the limitless potential that lies within our imaginations is lost to us

♦ imagination is denied being worthy of consideration as a talent to develop.

This is a deep misunderstanding. Daydreaming is never a waste of time, it is a highly advanced, adaptive faculty. When used properly, it is a very powerful human attribute. Original and creative thoughts form only in the imagination, are a crucial component of intuition, and form the basis of development of the human race. Each human society is based on intuitive dreams, imaginative thoughts and creative ideas, which then become a reality. We would still be living in caves if we did not have the imagination to develop and create as a species.

> *Intuition is the highest form of intelligence.* Albert Einstein

Just think of the implications of this: your mind, your thoughts, can create whatever your imagination can conceive of, and turn it into a reality. This is a principle. It does not work here and not there. It does not work for one person and not the next. It works, period (see box below). Knowing how it works is the key to using this attribute to its fullest potential.

This chapter asks you to value and develop your imagination as one of the most important skills and abilities you have in life. You cannot create your own reality if you cannot imagine it first. Start playing and exploring with your imagination. See how it influences your beliefs. Examine how they in turn influence your life and the reality you want to create for yourself.

First steps

Using your imagination and your mind to be creative works on the premise that you must:

◆ First become more aware of who you are, of all that you say, do and believe.

◆ Then be prepared to make changes where it limits and blocks you.

◆ Use this clarity to recognise what you really want in your life and create it.

This process can be applied to everything. Whether you believe it or not, it is influencing your life every moment right now.

What is a principle?

A principle is a general rule of life. It is as it is. A principle cannot have favourites, cannot work in this way and not in another, and cannot be adapted to suit our demands. A good example of this is the way coloured paints and dyes combine to make new colours. If we mix yellow and blue, they make green. Different amounts of yellow and blue make different shades of green but it is still green. We cannot decide that yellow and blue can only make green on Sundays or in the winter, they will always make green. It will not work for only Mary but not Jack, it works for whoever mixes them. However, if we mix yellow and blue and then unintentionally add a little red, we do not get green, we get something else. This is the same with your thoughts. You must make sure you are only mixing yellow and green and not adding red unintentionally. *So we must learn to recognise all the colours of our thoughts and how to keep them separate.*

Selecting your area of change

While you are still developing and practising this approach to living, choose an aspect of your life to change, adapt, or develop that is not too difficult to work with. You can come back to the others later. Choose an example from the following:

- ◆ mastery of a specific skill
- ◆ achieving a specific goal
- ◆ work
- ◆ self-esteem
- ◆ friendship
- ◆ relationships
- ◆ home
- ◆ health
- ◆ abundance (what we need in any area, eg money, comfort, all the above list, our sense of overall well-being).

Take time to develop these skills on smaller things in your life, because learning how to get it right is part of the 'getting it better in the future' process. Starting to consciously work on things that are more straightforward to accomplish, and work upwards, helps to build trust and understanding of how powerful this approach to life is.

Keeping everything positive

If we only think in terms of what we lack in life, or what we cannot do, we are continuously affirming what we do not have or what we fear. And we create that reality for ourselves because it becomes the internal window through which we view the world. We need to reframe that window, to see the positive in everything that exists. We can say which areas are not fulfilling us, but at the same time acknowledge what is good about them.

> Seeing the cup as half full, not half empty, helps us to acknowledge and value all we have.

Mapping your thoughts

Look at the *areas of change* listed above:

- ◆ Make a note of what you have already – be specific. See example in Figure 1.
- ◆ What is good and what is not so good? See Figure 2.
- ◆ What have both these aspects taught you, given that nothing in life lacks a positive dimension? See Figure 3.

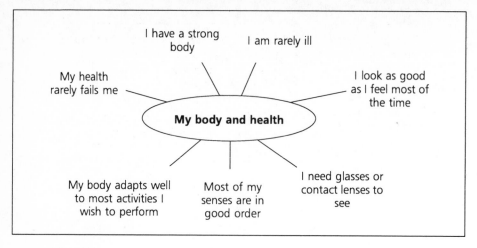

Fig. 1. Affirming the positive.

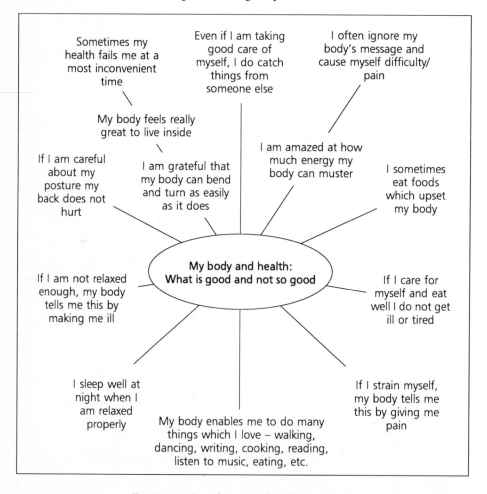

Fig. 2. Assessing what is good and not so good.

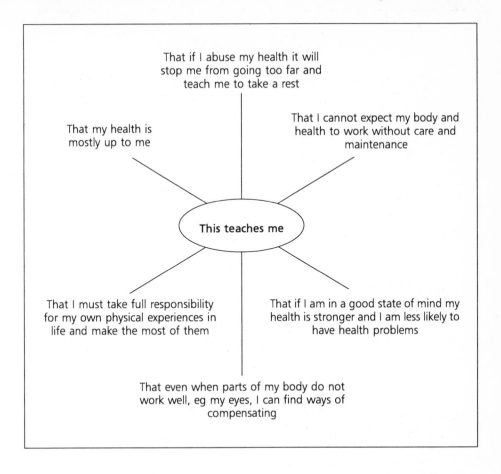

That if I abuse my health it will stop me from going too far and teach me to take a rest

That I cannot expect my body and health to work without care and maintenance

That my health is mostly up to me

This teaches me

That I must take full responsibility for my own physical experiences in life and make the most of them

That if I am in a good state of mind my health is stronger and I am less likely to have health problems

That even when parts of my body do not work well, eg my eyes, I can find ways of compensating

Fig. 3. Learning through the experiences.

Find a format that works for you in terms of illustrating your thoughts. If you are more of a word person you might like to write it out. Do this in a pictorial format such as a spidergram, as in the examples. If you are more visually orientated, create symbols or collages of images which work for you. Use your notebook for recording this.

> The most important thing is to recognise a positive aspect to every difficulty or problem we have to face. These positives can be in what they teach us, as we meet the challenge.

We address the importance of positive perceptions and interpretations to everything in Chapters 4, 5 and 6.

What do I really want?

So you have decided what you really want. Now break that down into what that represents in your life. You need to be very honest or you are in danger of 'muddying your colours' with conflicting beliefs and attitudes.

For instance, do you want money? Ask yourself these questions:

1   What does money represent: status, respect, security, a chance to try out a project or a business idea, a chance to fulfil a dream of doing something in your life? What else can you think of?

2   If you want money, where is this currently missing in your life: at home, at work, in your social or extended family groups?

3   If it is to fulfil a dream, has there ever been a chance you could have gone for this opportunity in any other way? Have you avoided it or decided you couldn't do it for some reason? Do you limit your own possibilities?

4   What is the best way to meet your true need, eg will money ever give you respect or security, will it make any difference at all, could it create other problems without solving the needs you want to fulfil? If it is a project, did you use money as an excuse to procrastinate doing it before, so will you take the opportunity if it arises again?

5   Is this the best way to meet that need, eg if you want respect and security, when did money ever do anything other than create an illusion of these attributes? How come some people have lots of both without having lots of money? If it is the opportunity then can you be sure you have the other qualities needed such as enthusiasm, perseverance? You might find it is not money you really want but an additional personal attribute which needs development. Which leads on to the next question.

6   What else could you do to meet this need? Having identified the root desire or dream underneath the perceived version, do you need to rethink and go back to the beginning or have you found you were right in

identifying your original dream and can now move on to the next stage?

Consider all your options and do not limit yourself to what you believe you can have or what your 'inner child' wants with a stamping foot. You may return to this stage after reading further.

> Remember, *all* your thoughts create *all* your realities.

Deciding what's important

This stage is very important. If you do not decide exactly *what* it is you want, you're likely to create something you *think* you want. You could find this is not bringing the satisfaction you expected. Taking time and care over each stage helps you to learn more about yourself and create your own life. Consider this statement and think how far you can apply it to your life:

◆ *There are no mistakes in life, ever, there are only lessons to be learned, and you are doing your very best with what you know at any given time.*

Whatever you get wrong this time, do it differently and learn from your mistakes. They are the richest resource you have for getting it right next time. The important thing is to keep working at getting things better. Do not give up on this because if you want to move on in life you must work at it; if you want to stay stuck then do nothing and you will stay there until something happens to force you to move on.

One way or another we do move on eventually and only we can choose how to do it, either openly or with a struggle. Most of our struggles are a result of our unwillingness to look at what we are doing now and see if there is a better way to do it next time. This is the true meaning of the word education, *educare* – to draw out – meaning to learn from within, from your own experiences and feelings. The school system has little to do with education. It offers knowledge, but knowledge is meaningless without experiences to teach its true importance. Learning means understanding something from within one's own experience.

Avoiding contradictions

Sometimes we say 'I want this thing in my life', and then say we don't really, just in case it doesn't happen. Hedging bets is not being creative or trusting but it is a common device of the ego.

It is important to recognise that what we want may come clothed in another format to the one expected. We should not try to control the manner of delivery of our wishes but leave them to be free to unfold as they will for our highest good.

> Be very clear and consistent about what you want, and remain open to how it manifests.

However, there is nothing you can't have as long as it does not come at the expense of anyone else, eg promotion at work must be because someone else has gone onto something better for them; a more beautiful garden must not be at the expense of the natural world.

What I believe – rejecting limitation

This is about what we believe we are entitled to have. We often feel there's no point in wanting something because it won't ever happen. It won't with that attitude: that is called **resistance**. It comes back to our thoughts and reality being our responsibility.

Recognising resistance

Resistance has many guises but for most people it comes in the form of voices, words or thoughts, often presented as 'common sense' or pragmatism. These represent what we believe on deeply held and assumed levels, without challenge. It is often a key basis for our blocks. Look at the following list and see which is your resistance guise.

- ◆ I do not deserve this.
- ◆ It is not acceptable to want this.
- ◆ I am selfish, greedy to want this.
- ◆ I am unrealistic to want/expect this.
- ◆ I cannot want what others have.
- ◆ It is better to accept what I have and not consider working

for improvement.

◆ I cannot have if others do not have.

◆ I am only allowed a certain amount.

◆ If I aim too high I will only be disappointed.

◆ If I expect good things I will only be disappointed when I get less.

◆ I should accept what life gives me and not seek to improve it in any way for myself.

◆ There are some who have and some who have not in this life.

◆ I have no control in my life so there's no point in trying for anything.

◆ There is not enough to go round.

◆ If everybody wanted more then we would have total destruction of the planet.

◆ There are winners and losers in life.

◆ My karma for this life is to suffer/be poor/remain unfulfilled.

You may have others. List your own resistance and limitation voices.

Creating your own reality

We create our own reality and always get what we ask for. So if we want something but believe we cannot have it or do it, for what ever reason, then that will be the case. It is as simple as that, but not for the reasons we first think. It is not because *life* is like that. It is because our *thoughts* are like that.

Why do you think that you should be allowed to have your wish come true? Recap on your heart's desire. For instance, if you want more money in your life ask yourself the following questions and create spidergrams for each of them. Some of these questions may seem to be repetitions of earlier ones but remember the importance of clarity; we want clear green not muddy sludge.

(a) Why do I want money? What do I actually want, that this would bring me?

(b) What are my beliefs about money:

- ◆ Does it last?
- ◆ Is it good to have money?
- ◆ Is it something to be guilty about when others do not have?
- ◆ Can money be trusted?
- ◆ Can I trust myself with money?
- ◆ Will concerns about money hold me back or work to support me?

(c) Why am I afraid of having more money in my life:

- ◆ What might it confront me with that I am unable to cope with – greed, jealousy?
- ◆ How might other people treat me?
- ◆ Will I fear losing it?
- ◆ Will I fear spending it in case it runs out?
- ◆ Does money mean unhappiness?
- ◆ What problems have I had in the past with money?

(d) What do I think about other people with money? Are they:

- ◆ Stuck in ruts, lucky, free, tied down, rich and unhappy?
- ◆ Unable to enjoy what they have because of fear of losing it?
- ◆ Spending most of it on protecting what they have?

(e) What are the advantages of *not* having this change in my life; what would the change require me to give up that I cherish:

- ◆ Do I see myself as poor and honest?
- ◆ Do I like to avoid responsibility?
- ◆ Would I have to stop complaining about lack of time/money/opportunity?
- ◆ Would I have to stop finding excuses and justifications for not doing things?
- ◆ Would I have to give up my previous beliefs about security?

(f) What benefit would more money bring to others around me:

- ◆ Can I use this opportunity to benefit others with my work, offer employment, provide a valuable service?
- ◆ Will my family benefit from this opportunity as much as

me?
- Will my increased fulfillment in life make me less grumpy?
- Will it finally enable me to allow for the needs of others and not feel resentful?

Allow your thoughts to come through with each of these six spidergrams or collages. If possible discuss them with a trusted friend or partner who listens and does not tell you what to do or think. Especially avoid talking it through with people who dismiss or diminish your thoughts. Share your ideas and think about them: is it what you really feel? Until you work out what you really feel you cannot create what you want because you might be blocking it. This is dealt with later.

Summary

We all have the capacity to create the life we want but it is a skill that needs to be recognised and developed.
- Use your imagination as often and as freely as you can.
- Developing techniques which put you in control of your own thoughts is a powerful tool in creating your chosen reality.
- These techniques are based on universal principles, so learn to use them to your advantage.
- Examine what you really want in your life and quietly work towards it, knowing it will happen when you allow it to.

Affirmations are powerful tools for creating change in our lives, when we use them constructively.

Playing with Affirmations

An affirmation is a statement of intent. We all use affirmations daily, both consciously and unconsciously, either spoken out loud or silently in our heads. Affirmations are an important activity for consciously creating your life. They are powerful tools for creating change and development if they are used constructively.

Until we know and understand how powerful affirmations are, we tend to use them unconsciously. We do not recognise how they are affecting our lives all the time. They also tell us a lot about ourselves:

◆ They illustrate the deeply held beliefs we hold about ourselves, life, and other people.
◆ They create predictions about our intentions for our future.
◆ They show whether our perception tends to be negative or positive.

The most important task here is to recognise and understand exactly what affirmations are and how we can use them to our advantage.

Affirmations create the *energy of change*. The trouble is that we often follow them by thinking that it should occur immediately. A thought is a very light form of energy and it takes some time to create enough momentum to manifest itself into the material or emotional world of human experience. But as soon as you have made an affirmation you have created that energy. The delay is an illusion that makes us think it has not occurred. If we give power to that illusion we negate the original creative energy. This is a complicated concept so this chapter breaks it down in stages.

What are we saying now? Inner dialogues

For most of us there is a constant chatter of thoughts running through our minds. Most of these thoughts are unspoken and we are often unaware of them. Sometimes we may even start to speak out loud to ourselves, vocalising this inner chatter, rather like Shirley Valentine. This is our mind talking to itself, our **stream of consciousness,** and it can create several difficulties:

1   It can feel as if we have no control over it. This chatter is our worst enemy in terms of living peacefully and 'muddying the colours' for us.

2   It is blocking your access to the higher, deeper and wiser thoughts which are the greater part of your consciousness. The hill blocks the view of the mountain.

3   It can make you lose touch with those wiser thoughts and believe you do not have any.

4   This thought train is influential in creating your present reality.

We should and can have control over this voice (often called the voice of the ego) but first we must notice it and what it is saying.

Try it now

Over the next few days and/or weeks start listening to your inner voice as if you are listening to someone else. Stay as detached and uninvolved with the contents as you can. If you find yourself involved with the dialogue just detach your self repeatedly, until you find detachment automatic. First make a list of the topics and perceptions of this inner chatter. Then look at how it is saying this.

Notice especially:

◆ Are most of the topics about the past, the present or the future as you 'see' it?

◆ Do they seem to be mostly about grievances or slights against you?

◆ Do they take you to happy thoughts and memories?

◆ Do they seem to be mostly optimistic and planning ahead?

◆ What emotions do you feel as these thoughts run through your mind?

◆ Are they constructive and helpful?

◆ Are they showing you how you can change and grow – what you can learn?

- ◆ Are they feelings and thoughts of revenge?
- ◆ Are they thoughts that say 'this is too hard/much/far'?
- ◆ Are they thoughts and feelings of injustices against you?
- ◆ Are they justifications for your own inappropriate/self-limiting behaviours?
- ◆ Can you tell them to hush up?
- ◆ Do you feel unable to stop them?
- ◆ Do you argue with them sometimes?
- ◆ Do you encourage them sometimes?
- ◆ Do you enjoy them at all/feel justified in their content/gain some pleasure or satisfaction from them?
- ◆ Do you feel irritated if someone interrupts you in the middle of them?
- ◆ Are they repetitive – returning to the same themes?
- ◆ Are they self-defeating voices like 'you'll never do it', or 'you can't do that'?
- ◆ How does your body feel as these thoughts run through – calm or tense?
- ◆ Do they change tack and argue back at you or convince you of their 'rightness'?

Notice anything else about them that you can. Look more and more closely each time you explore.

The exercise above is a form of mindfulness and requires a great deal of honesty. You may find voices you dislike and do not want to admit to. You may have to admit you are stuck in old thought patterns which no longer apply. Denying their existence will be counter-productive to your creative visualisation process if it is to work as effectively as possible for you.

Recognising the light

Negative thoughts are based in our fear. Fear is rather like a shadow. It has no real substance and no basis in truth unless we believe in it. There is nothing to struggle with except our belief in that fear. So we struggle with our self.

> Like shadows, our fears disappear when we turn and face them with the light of recognition.

Releasing negative and unconscious thought trains is as easy as turning on a light once we know that is all we have to do. The light in this case is changing to positive affirmations and developing a quiet mind.

Getting our thoughts out into the open is very important if we are to deal with them and get them saying what we really want. So make a comprehensive list of all these thoughts, starting with the most dominant ones.

Taming the mind

Taming the mind is usually much easier said than done. People who want to start meditating regularly often find the 'voices' are the hardest blocks to overcome. But meditation and using taped visualisations are excellent ways of getting the mind used to working differently and training it. There are a couple of stages involved in mastering it, like the above exercise, and it does take determination and sticking power. But with regular and intentional determined effort you will achieve the quieting.

Taking the detached approach is a good way of loosening the mind's power and control over you. Start with short and regular periods of meditation, from 30 seconds to two minutes at a time and repeat ten times each day. Set a special time aside each day when you will allow yourself to stay in meditation for longer and stick to it. Start with five minutes and gradually build this up to ten, 15, 30 minutes, longer if you want. It is not the length of time that really matters but the quality of your relaxation. All this kind of mind work is a process of letting go of old mental bad habits and learning to go into our own mind calmly and peacefully – to reclaim conscious control of what our thoughts really are and what they are doing to your life.

Recognising past thought patterns

Look at your list of unintentional affirmations you have been making regularly in your chattering mind thought trains. How many came true in one way or another, even if you thought of them as just 'hope it doesn't happen' fear-based thought? You might begin to recognise yourself as the creator of your own reality now. If you keep reminding yourself of the principle that *thought creates reality*, you can begin to see how much this is true.

Affirming ourselves

How often do you stand in front of the mirror and think about yourself? When you do, how many voices are passing judgement on you? Look at your list and pick the ten most common thoughts you have. Are they positive or negative? If possible how could you develop them, eg:

I'm not a bad person really = I am as good as I can be at this moment
or
I'm quite good at... really = I am doing my best with what I know and I am improving constantly.

Trying out ways of making affirmations

Affirmations should always be expressed:
◆ in the present
◆ in positive terms.

So a good affirmation will simply state:

I am all that I need to be
or
Right here, right now everything is fine, all my needs are met.

These are very good examples to use as part of your daily meditation breaks.
But an affirmation like these:

I must stop getting up so late in the morning
I will try to do some exercise each day

will achieve little because they contain the expectation of either failure or procrastination, or both.
A better format for these two would be:
I wake each morning feeling refreshed and ready to enjoy the day.
Exercise forms a natural and joyful part of my daily routine.

Now try writing some affirmations for yourself and keep

checking how you write them. It is very easy to slip into accidental negatives but it must be kept *present* and it must be kept *positive.*

Make affirmations playfully

Affirmations are more powerful if they are spoken out loud to yourself. Doing it into a mirror increases this further, as long as you do it with serious intent, albeit allowing for a fun element. Who wouldn't have a bit of a giggle when talking to themselves very seriously in the mirror? Have fun with affirmations, play with them.

One way is to clap it into a clapping song against your own hands in the mirror. Then you are using three senses: sight, touch and hearing. This has the effect of creating an image and intention with both sides of the brain, both the ego-based logical left brain and the intuitive, sensitive creative right side. If you add a feel-good fun factor it should lodge in your limbic system too, which is the emotional brain.

Try these other ways of affirming so that it becomes incorporated into your daily life in a positive and conscious way.

1　Say your affirmations to a friend and get the friend to reaffirm – doing this for each other is a lovely gift in friendship.

2　Ask a friend to make the affirmations to you randomly during the day/week – this is very useful for overcoming any old negative failure programmes you were taught as a child.

3　Say them as a prayer before you go to sleep at night.

4　Say them as a mantra during a meditation.

5　Write them out like school lines to yourself and pin it up somewhere.

6　Make a collage of ideas relating to your affirmation and hang it somewhere prominent so you can be reminded of it regularly.

7　Use affirmations in conversation eg 'I am...'

8   Sing, chant, or make rhymes out of your affirmations.

> *There is but one cause of human failure and that is man's lack of faith in his true self.* William James

Checking for limitation beliefs

Are there any parts of you that are still objecting to your wishes coming true? Do you feel quite comfortable with this or is any voice still saying who are you kidding? These objectors are actually trying to protect you but they may well be coming from your **ego**, loosely termed, **earth guide only**; we are talking about being creative from our **inner selves**, or our higher, spiritual selves, whatever term you are comfortable with. So it is our higher selves we need to consult for this wish to come true (see next chapter).

Limitations are blocks in our awareness of the 'light always being on'. They are the things that convince us we are still living in the shadows. Blocks occur because we are closed spiritually, mentally, emotionally, physically or sexually. And once we have a block it is like a log jam, it traps everything behind it and gradually builds up to proportions which far outweigh the original block and its motivation for closure.

Casual closures of positive beliefs

We might have had a hope dashed in childhood by being told that dreams don't come true. Perhaps it was said to us by a well-meaning adult who did not realise the power of their words. From a simple denial of our childhood beliefs, we have unconsciously ceased to believe in our own potential. We trusted the words of someone who also did not understand the implications of what they were saying and had probably been given the same belief in their childhood and had merely passed it on. Because it had become the self-fulfilling prophesy, their belief system and therefore their reality, they believed they were saving you from unnecessary disappointment.

Being is a state of mind

It is important to understand the difference between *having* something or *being* something. The former is possession and the latter is an expression of your attributes. For instance, if you take a course of study what is your motivation? Will your whole goal be to obtain the qualification and the status that it brings, or is it the experience the course offers in terms of stretching and developing you that counts more? Is having the qualification more important, or being open to the experiences that come with the course?

Behaviour, or 'doing', is based on the original motivation. If your goal is to be rich for its own sake you are in a 'having' mode, and therefore your 'doing' will be governed by that. If on the other hand your intention is to have all your needs met, to make progress and try out new things in life, to be content, then your action will occur accordingly. Many people believe they have to 'do' something to prove their worth. Being allows you to value yourself for your intrinsic worth, without needing to prove anything.

> *Lives based on having are less free than lives based either on doing or being.* William James

Many people still believe that they firstly need to have in order to be, eg they need to *have* money and then they will *be* happy. Or they believe that it is impossible to be happy or an honest person if you are rich. The truth is that you must first *be* contented or happy with who you are and then *be* contented and happy with the idea of material comfort, then you can *have* money and material comfort in a fulfilling way.

So being first, then doing, leads to having in a way that is comfortable and enhances happiness.

If you do it the other way round you have the opposite effect: you find that the more you have the less happy or content you are. Abundance or wealth in itself is neutral. It cannot make you anything that you are not already but it will magnify it.

> *A person who is not disturbed by the incessant flow of desires*
> *– that enters like rivers into the ocean, which is ever being*
> *filled but is always still – can alone achieve peace, and not*
> *the man who strives to satisfy such desires. Bhagavad Gita*

Unblocking your creativity

The next step is to actively release your blockages. This can be
done with affirmations, meditations and expressed desired
intentions. We continue to address this in greater depth in later
chapters through the development of self-knowledge.

For instance, as all negative thought and feeling has its roots
in fear, we should try to analyse the nature of that fear.
Fear is False Evidence Appearing Real.

A simple affirmation will do. Write your own because this is
more meaningful to you, but some ideas are:
- I allow my imagination to explore all possibilities.
- I release all beliefs in limitation.
- I open myself to my full potential.

Be careful to avoid limiting affirmations such as:
- I want this job because it gives me more money and
responsibility.
- I want to write songs for my friends and family to hear.

Both of these immediately limit how far you are allowing
yourself to go. Instead affirm:
- I want a job that leads me to fulfil my potential in the best
possible way.
- I want to write songs that will be enjoyed by anyone in the
world who wants to hear them.

Start your affirmation reprogramming with some positive
affirmations about yourself and the one thing we could all use
more of.
- I am a *loved and loving* person.
- I release all fear of *love and rejection*.
- I invite *new love* to come into my life.

- I am open to *love, loving another* unconditionally, and *being loved* unconditionally in return.
- I open myself to receiving *love* in all the forms it can show itself, for my highest good.
- I open myself to my own infinite capacity *to love and be loved.*

These are all suggestion but you should try writing or creating your own affirmations; just remember to stick to the rules:
- Keep it completely positive.
- Keep it in the present.

For further developments, the words in italics above can be replaced with your own specific requirements eg, garden, skill, holiday, career, money, etc. Play with the format until it feels right for you.

Summary

If your mind and your thoughts create reality, finding positive and constructive ways of changing thought patterns is essential for creating the life you want to live.
- Check your thoughts by monitoring them consciously, objectively and intentionally.
- Notice how much you have created your present with your thoughts.
- Learn and develop skills and techniques for quieting the mind and freeing it from unwanted thoughts.
- Develop a range of clearing affirmations to deal with blocks and limitation beliefs.

CHAPTER 4

Understanding the True Nature of the Ego

When we hear the word **ego** we tend to think of someone being too full of themselves, too proud or vain, too full of self-importance. We see them as waiting for a fall.

The term ego has been used within many different paradigms of psychology. A paradigm is a model or framework used as a means of interpreting information to form a recognisable pattern. Ego comes from the Latin for 'I am', so it is used to summarise a concept of 'who we are' in human psychological terms.

When the ego is referred to in spiritual psychologies, such as metaphysics and Buddhism, it takes on a slightly different meaning. For people looking at their development holistically, the ego represents the exclusively human part of our true reality. We are humans and have a human experience of reality, but we are also much more than that. As we become more acquainted with our human reality, it helps us to discover more of our true nature. The whole self.

So what is the ego? What role does it play in our lives?

Knowing the self

Self-awareness is not the same as self-importance, centredness, or selfishness. Self-awareness means:

♦ Knowing yourself sufficiently to anticipate your responses to other people and experiences.
♦ Knowing what your motivation is, why you feel like that.
♦ Being able to choose how to respond in any given situation.

Self-centredness and selfishness means someone:

♦ Only sees the world in terms of their own needs being met.
♦ Cannot take into consideration how their behaviour affects others.

◆ Expects what they want to take precedence over what others might feel.
◆ Being less able to choose and recognise their own behaviour.

We are all a combination of the above, depending on how self-aware we are and our experiences in life.

> This is what it means to be responsible for one's own life: *to be able to make the response you would choose, given the information you have, to obtain the outcomes you would prefer.*

Being responsible means able to make a response. This means:
◆ Not reacting automatically.
◆ Not assuming things are 'as they always have been'.
◆ Not basing the present solely on past experience.
◆ Not making sweeping assumptions about other people's intentions from your perspective.
◆ Not allowing old grievances to influence the way you feel now.
◆ Accepting that we all make mistakes in life and we can all learn from them.
◆ Not forgetting that the only moment that exists is the everlasting now.

Psychological perspectives

As a human we have an ego. This is part of our individual identity and personality. When Sigmund Freud made one of the earliest attempts at identifying the personality he divided it into three components:
◆ the **id**
◆ the **ego**
◆ the **superego**.

The id

The id is an instinct-driven, basic animal and survival needs energy, which desires gratification of libido or life energy. It is present at birth and is basically *I want now*. Libido as the life force does not only refer to sexual drive, as we tend to use it, but to all drives for survival. Food and shelter are part of the urge to survive and procreate. For most of us work represents the need to provide for ourselves and our children. Many people would not work as they do if they only had their own basic needs to consider. Some people consider needs differently from others; one person's need is a non-essential to another and a luxury to a third. So the desire to have a successful career, and a certain house, is only an extension of the basic id drive. The id is also the basis for competition, competing for one's own needs to be met and one's own prowess to be noticed. Finally the id is the basis for aggression as a means of securing one's needs.

The ego

The ego develops in a child at around 18 months old and represents the practical reality of the environment, and the people who inhabit our lives. It is seen as the civilising influence of our id nature. It develops as we learn that our desires are not instantly gratified by those around us: 'I want now but I will have to wait a little while'. If we do not like the model of reality we are presented with, we develop ego defences. Freud identified several including:

◆ repression
◆ fixation
◆ regression
◆ identification.

Fixation occurs when we do not develop beyond a trauma, and we are stuck. Although it is over in experiential terms, it is still continuing inside our perception. Fixation can also occur when over-indulgence has failed to equip us with sufficient empathy to consider the needs of others, eg over-indulgence of the id – the 'spoiled child'.

The superego

According to Freud, the superego develops around age 4 to 5 but it differs in individual children. This is often called conscience, morals and values, or the internalised parent. If the superego is over-developed it is the basis for shame, guilt and self-limiting thought patterns. An under-developed superego results in a lack of moral values and guilt, and therefore no restriction to the urges of the id, leading to irresponsible and possibly amoral and antisocial behaviours. Both cause the ego considerable difficulty in balancing them with the urges of the id.

Superego develops from an ego defence called identification: someone else has what we want or perceive we need and we identify with them. By becoming like them we can achieve/ acquire their successes. We adopt their values, plus social and cultural values, and assimilate them into our personal value system.

Balancing inner forces

Freud believed it is the healthy balance between these three forces that makes our personality stable. A strong ego and calm superego will enable a comfortable life with the id safely catered for and controlled. He also believed that we seek to find others with whom we can identify through our ego – people who share the same values and outlook on life. This allows us to feel comfortable with, and justify, our attitudes, goals and experiences. The superego manifests in any authority with whom we invest the power to influence us. We then become obedient to that authority and its values.

Ego development

Freud's work has received much criticism and it is insufficient alone to interpret the complexity of human experience, but it does begin to form a framework of understanding about the human mind and concepts of reality. Eric Erikson, who trained with Anna Freud, took the idea of ego development further, differentiating it into specific tasks of learning at certain stages and ages.

Each stage is a development of the previous one. Strengths develop from either comfortable or challenging, painful experiences. We learn through the contrasts and have to experience pleasant and unpleasant examples in order to fully

Stage	Age	Feature	Relationships	Human values
1	0–1	basic trust *v* mistrust	mother/principal carer	hope – belief
2	1–3	autonomy *v* shame/doubt	parents/care group	willpower
3	3-6	initiative *v* guilt	basic family	purpose
4	7–12	industry/inferiority	social environment /school	competence
5	12–18	identity *v* role confusion	peers, social groups, leaders	fidelity/loyalty
6	20s	intimacy *v* isolation	partners and close friends	love
7	30–50	generativity *v* stagnation	household sharing/work	care
8	50 on	ego integrity *v* despair	all humankind	wisdom

master each stage. Full mastery of the feature is required for flexibility of response and fluid ability to live life as it comes. Lack of mastery of any of these stages results in rigid, repetitive reactions over which we have very little control. That is the basis for being stuck in our life. For instance, being stuck with trust issues means we have difficulty mastering trust in its fullness, so we :

◆ trust inappropriately
◆ fail to trust enough
◆ fail to trust our self
◆ fail to be trustworthy.

We explore issues of trust in depth later.

Archetypes and egos

Carl Jung saw the ego as essential to human experience, that without it we would metaphorically die as an individual. But he took a far broader approach to the reality of consciousness. Jung concluded it was the lack of connection with our own individual spiritual natures that causes all our problems in society and on a personal level.

Jung talked about **archetypes**, ideals embodied in a persona or character to which we relate, for instance Hercules the hero; Mary the good mother figure; the wicked witch etc. He suggested God was a concept that was ultimately unknowable but part of the general archetypes, the models of reality as we think it should be. Most of us hold these ideals within our consciousness as a benchmark for our performance.

Archetypes include magical beings and are encountered through myth, story, art, dreams and religions. It is their qualities that make them an archetype. These are the unconscious role models by which we judge ourselves. Self is the central archetype of our own unique and individual potentials. In this respect the whole self is divided into two dimensions:

> ↗ Life goals and self-healing based on archetype ideals

Whole self

> ↘ Emerging and developing capacity to reach those ideals and assimilate them into our sense of self.

Jung divides the mind into:

◆ **Conscious** – the thoughts we have.
◆ **Unconscious** – buried and unrevealed except through dreams and underlying beliefs or unintentional and unexpected behaviours.
◆ **Collective unconscious** – race consciousness, the accumulation of all common thought energies into a recognisable force in people's minds. Jung defines this as a field of spiritual energy containing the archetypes. These are inherited or instinctual mental frameworks and concepts, paradigms that carry potentials, ie it can be seen as positive or negative according to perception but is of itself neutral.

Within this latter we find personal reference points for our roles in life, the archetypes of sister, father, daughter etc. These are the basis of our self-assessment and self-image – how well do we fit our own archetypes and how much do we question these models we have?

Models of harmony

Potentials for harmony include disharmony, on a two-dimensional model, with balance in the centre (see Figure 4), eg God is harmony/devil is disharmony – same archetype, different dimensions of same influence in our life. These include social and cultural norms, and expectations of who we are and how we develop, how special qualities are valued or denied in each society. For instance clairvoyancy is seen as a great gift in some cultures and families but as cranky in western materialistic society. Individual spirituality may be seen as different or deviant, but Christianity as conforming to one social norm of a good citizen.

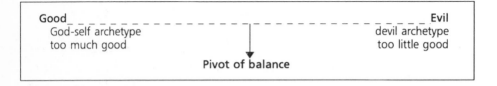

Fig. 4. Role of ego to create best choices for self.

Ego is the centre of the conscious mind. We have already suggested one acronym that helps put it into perspective: ego: Earth Guide Only. Another acronym is Easing God Out, meaning pushing us away from the God within, your spiritual self. Separating you from your whole self is what creates vulnerability to fear. The ego is clearly against your spiritual reunion with your whole self. It is the human self only and it wants to take over. (See Figure 5.)

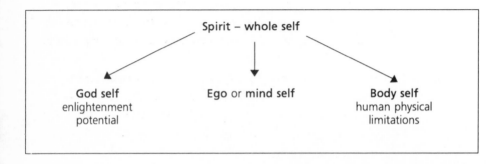

Fig. 5. Aspects of the whole self.

Identities of self

One of the ways in which we define our self and gain a sense of self is through our roles and relationships. These are based on archetypes or models of what we expect from that relationship. What is the structure we have imposed on that relationship? What are the ideal qualities, the social status, the skills and achievements associated with that relationship or role?

Try it now   Write a list of all the roles you have in life (parent, sibling, teacher, employee, customer, the list is endless). What qualities do you expect from each of these roles?

Each role carries responsibilities and expectations for the successful role fulfilment. For instance the role of parent, depending on which gender, might have variations on the following themes: trustworthy, supportive, nurturing, forgiving, teaching, giving guidance and values, loyal, sharing and caring, sharing and providing property and material wealth, supporting education and career, prioritising it above own needs, always providing best intentions for you as an individual.

This might be your idealised parent archetype, but your real experience might be different. The value you place on your experiences with your parents, and perhaps of being a parent, will be judged on the criteria of your ideal.

Aspects of experience

There are two principles to state here:
- ◆ **Mirroring** – recognising the impersonal nature of everything. All that happens in life is a demonstration of what we hold on to in our conscious and unconscious minds, together with what we adopt unquestioningly from the collective unconscious.
- ◆ **Self knowledge** or **internal referencing**. No one can permanently affect or upset you, or have any power over you, if you do not hold it as a belief within you that their truth is greater than your own.

Who am I?

Consider to what extent you are what others make you – either directly or indirectly: parents, newspapers, propaganda, advertisers, partners, colleagues:

◆ Am I living for self or others – internal or external referencing?

◆ Am I wanting or depending on approval from others?

◆ Am I 'committing suicide' in a relationship?

◆ Am I listening to other people's opinions rather than my own?

◆ Is my identity based on relationships?

◆ Do I meet my own needs – become my own refuge? Who can meet those needs?

◆ How much of yourself is actually living up to others' expectations of you?

◆ Have you ever stopped wearing something because someone commented on it?

Many people adopt patterns of behaviour because they believe they please other people. Can we ever be happy trying to achieve what others want of us, especially if our self-esteem is based on someone else's view of us, given that they have their own agendas and lessons to learn? Living up to others' expectations of us is an impossible goal because what people say they want and what they really want from us are rarely the same.

◆ The boss will not want us to be successful.

◆ The mother will want us to be there all the time.

◆ One's partner will want us to behave as they require.

Are we living up to an image of someone who is not really there and ignoring the person who is there: our whole self? We often do not know who we are inside and this is the starting point for all of us (see Figure 6). Until we undertake this task we are usually left with a fixed sense of self that is rigid, full of attachments, based on other people's values and not our own.

If we relate the self to certain roles, what do we sacrifice to achieve these roles? How do the changing perceptions of society as a whole determine who we are? Am I my car, my house, my job, the newspaper I read, my partner, clothes I wear?

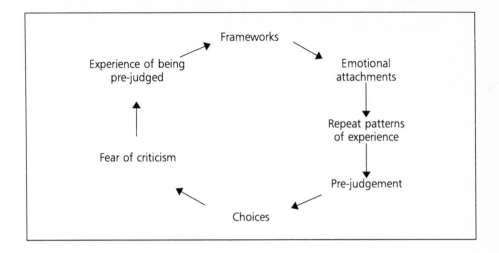

Fig. 6. The structuring of self – creating reality.

Try it now   Sit quietly for about 15 minutes with closed eyes and think about the statement below. If your mind wanders then bring it back with gentle determination. Give this single thought your fullest attention. Consider its implications in your own life, and in the lives of those around you.

I can be equal to anyone if I am not in competition with them. The most blessed person is the one most at peace with themselves.

Accepting the unknowable

There will always be a part of ourselves that we do not know consciously. There comes a stage when standing apart from 'oneself' (and here we are stuck with the limitations of words), one has to accept that we are subject to emotions triggered externally, without recourse to conscious perception. As such our own task is to skilfully manage the feelings that our mind presents us with. To feel guilt or shame, anger or fear, as a result of such emotional outpouring is not skilful. To deny or repress these feelings is self-damaging and pointless. We must learn to accept that something has triggered an emotion or set of emotions and presented us with an image of ourselves with which we are uncomfortable:

◆ this is not the self I want
◆ here is an opportunity to change
◆ here is the positive outcome of the negative.

Often the real difficulty is in identifying why such emotions have risen to the surface. When we cannot accept the reason, we panic and become depressed, leading to a downward spiral. The mistake is in believing that you are directly responsible for these thoughts. You are only responsible for your response to them and how you deal with them in the future.

> You are only responsible for actions taken consciously, for it is only these actions over which you have control.

Skilful decisions will lead to positive and comfortable outcomes, unskilful decisions lead to further discomfort until we master the lesson we are being shown.

Confronting the ego

The ego gives us all our problems. If we existed without our ego we would be existing in pure love and we would be free from human difficulties. It is the exclusively human part of our minds and therefore of us, but not our true nature, so the term Earth Guide Only applies very well.

◆ Ego is a guide to the challenges we will all overcome eventually, in order to return to the truth about our real identity and our real value.
◆ Whilst we have to overcome it, ego is not our enemy, we have to integrate it.
◆ Ego is a spiritual challenger and will catch us out if we allow it.
◆ Ego is there to test us and push us towards spiritual truth by its own failures, even though it appears to desire our continued captivity in a human reality of lack and limitation.
◆ Ego makes us value what we achieve in our consciousness, to recognise the quality of life experience that dawns as we begin to wake up to who we really are.
◆ Ego tests our resolve and therefore ultimately strengthens us in our quest for full self-awareness without selfishness.

We cannot experience the lessons of humanhood without some aspect of ego also coming into play.

Did you see the *Superman* film where a computer gains a sense of its own power and starts taking over, growing far beyond what was ever intended? The ego is rather like that. It is a tool of human consciousness but, if we allow it, it becomes very powerful and persuades us that this is all that exists, that ego is our true nature, so it can seem as if the ego has control of us. It doesn't unless we choose to give it the power it finds so attractive, and we do this by believing in the illusions about fear.

Defences of the ego

Fear is the absence of complete love and therefore always in conflict with the higher spirit within us. The basis of the fight between god and the devil is not between heaven and hell out there, but the heaven and hell which exists in states of either fear or love within us. We lose contact with our higher sense of self and the true spiritual self and listen to the ego. The ego promotes ideas of:

- fear and limitation
- lack of love
- lack of whatever we need being available for us, as and when we need it
- it being foolish to espouse trust or belief
- desire for proof, evidence, insurance policies against the future because our needs might not be met
- spiritual superiority 'I know more about spirituality/god than they do', 'my religion is the right one'
- assumptions of goodness based on judgement of others
- shame of our mistakes in life and attempts to hide them from others, an inverted form of judgement
- tragic poses as the victim of life, refusing to forgive and accept
- cynical positions on aspects of belief, or demands of intellectual proof.

This is the voice of the ego. Do you recognise its power in your life right now? Consider how many things you could or might do if it were not for a voice of caution counselling you not to take risks, or trust that things will work out for the best.

So ego has all its power located in fear. And although in human form we cannot live without it completely, because it gives us an appearance of individuality, we can remove its power by recognising and mastering it.

There are various ways in which we can achieve that:

◆ Meditation, the art of letting go of conscious thought, which is where ego manifests.

◆ Prayer and contemplation of higher truths, the desire to learn and understand the spiritual and mystical teachings at a personal level.

◆ Working on our psychology and recognising all the layers of fear and the responses which come from it. As we work through our fears, and release and learn to live without them we are slowly reducing the power of the ego and allowing our higher self to come through.

> A rough guide to knowing when you have ego voices in control is anything that makes you feel less balanced and calm.

Not feeling totally joyful means that there is an ego voice involved at some level. This must be true because ego's opposite voice is love, which ultimately knows no fear.

Conquering the dictator

The difficulty with ego is, like most things with a lot of power, it doesn't want to lose it. The ego is a megalomaniac, a little dictator in your consciousness that keeps you living in fear. It creates imaginary fears that you believe are real, another version of the thought-creates-reality principle. You will argue that they are real because you have experience of the reality, but *your thoughts were there first*. You created this experience from your consciousness and the collective consciousness.

One individual can only change their own experience, but a collective can change whole social structures. Think of the French and Russian revolutions. Both started with a few people thinking differently, not accepting things as they were but deciding to consider alternatives for themselves and for everyone else. The real task is to master our ego thoughts and choose what to think for ourselves. If each individual takes responsibility for their contribution to the collective, nothing is impossible. Taking responsibility for your own contribution is crucial to creating a loving social reality for all. But start with yourself first. Master this and you will have done as much as anyone can ever do.

It is a process of self-mastery. Let's look at some of the above list in more depth.

Intellectual tactics

The intellectual approach is denying anything without proof, asking questions and looking for arguments or exceptions that appear to dispute universal truths. If you recognise that thought creates reality in its fullest sense, thoughts will always create a reality that can appear to contradict the principle for a while. Once you master the ego, you stop looking for proof outside your own consciousness and accept that the only proof we need is the proof of our own experience. Called **solipsism**, that is the only proof that exists in any real sense.

Permanence – nothing must change

Another attitude of the ego is 'nothing must change'. 'If everything stays the same, I can cope, I know what is happening, I am in control of my life'. Yet the truth is that we are never in control of our lives. We never know where we will be taken next and what we will be expected to learn next.

Control

The desire to control and keep things or people as we want, not as they want to be, suggests 'my model of reality is the right one'. It is based on judgements of good/bad or right/ wrong. But by whose criteria do we judge? And who are we – God? Yes, but the part of us that wants to control is not God consciousness.

Logic and rational thinking

Using rational and logical explanations of why things cannot be other than as they see it is another intellectual form of denial. Sometimes the explanations are much more far-fetched than the idea being denied, but because they conform to the preferred model of life they are seen as more probable. But on closer consideration they are clearly a desperate act, from a desperately frightened ego trying to hold on to its own model of reality and its belief in its own power.

Fashionably cynical

Cynicism is a fashionable position to take on things, similar to disdain and ridicule. Cynicism seeks to:

◆ make an idea look stupid
◆ make fun of it, to be witty and popularly clever
◆ reject, in case one appears wrong
◆ refute the possibility that there is a truth somewhere in what one is rejecting because it threatens the premise upon which you base your life.

As above, this is believing that you need to be right.

Mere emotions

Many people still think that intellect is more powerful than emotion. But it is the other way round. The intellect is useless without an emotional perspective on everything it tackles. Take street crime as an example; the purely intellectual logical argument is to execute anybody immediately they commit a crime and provide identity passes for everybody, but an immediately emotional response says this is an intrusion of freedom and unjust. Logically this would solve the problem of street crime but we *feel* outraged at the idea.

> Emotions guide the intellect towards making the best decisions, not the other way round.

The important thing is not to see either emotions or intellect in isolation but as a team which, when used together, help us through life choices most effectively. The intellect helps us see the choices we have, the emotions help us make the best choice. Using either emotions or intellect in isolation leads to making the biggest mistakes.

Desperation and hope

If thoughts create reality, thoughts with a powerful emotional aspect have the greatest creative potential. And a thought with very little emotion behind it has a weak creative energy potential. The strength of the emotion is not the only influence, we must have positive emotion behind a thought to give it maximum creative power. The most positive thought energy to have is trusting that what is best for us is what will happen anyway. So any form of desperation to create something in our life will destroy it. The ego device is to make us want things badly, to believe that if we only have this or that then we will find contentment. Hope is a negative because it suggests that it might not happen. It contradicts trust and belief.

Accepting the message of our mirror reflections

We do not see things as they are, we see things as *we* are. We are always subjective in our experiences because otherwise we would not respond to them, they trigger something inside us. The ego will take an experience and make it into a:
- 'that's out of order' or
- 'you can't trust that' or
- 'don't believe it's that good, nothing ever is'

and seek to deny our right to have or trust that our needs and hearts' desires are being met. The ego will start building up an argument from a position of anger and fear, or will deny our truth by challenging our perception. The truth is that everything around us is God, or universal energy, expressing itself. We are surrounded by the evidence that:
- we are in the universe and therefore connected to it and subject to it
- therefore we cannot be destroyed or hurt within the whole
- we will just change and become something new within the whole.

The ego would have us believe we are separate and therefore alone. This is the basis of our fear, a sense of isolation and aloneness when we should be feeling a sense of at-oneness.

Being blind to love

Based on judgements of good and bad, the ego teaches us:

◆ not to see all we have and recognise the love in it
◆ to see what we do not have, what we lack
◆ to believe we will find happiness through whatever it points its attention at next.

The ego will do everything it can to prevent us receiving love, a gift, anything that brings a sense of needs being met. So we see things as *we* are, not as *they* are. Your life experiences and ego perspectives will colour your interpretation of everything that happens in your life, and attract to you that which confirms your beliefs. In the same way we prefer the company of people who hold the same beliefs that we do, including our own self-worth, or lack of it. We find comfort in agreeing a common view of life's injustices, a 'them and us' approach, which is separation. We avoid taking responsibility for creating our own experiences and look for evidence to support our victim hypothesis.

Reframe your outlook on life

Look again at everything as evidence of love. Even if someone mistreats us, it is love because it is an opportunity to find your strength and grow, to learn and develop. One of the traps which ego often leads us into is justifying our right to be angry with somebody or with the world, to retaliate and take revenge, to be angry with someone for just being the way they are rather than how we want them to be. That is all ego perception because it is saying 'it's all out there'. It cannot be out there if it is not inside us.

◆ We cannot change the world until we can change inside of us.
◆ We cannot change other people we can only change our self.

The ego wants to fix other people. It thinks it can see what they need to do but blinds us to what we need to do. This is the basis for all the lessons we will learn.

Control and acceptance

The meaning of control is the desire to change what is outside ourselves without looking inside first: 'I can fix this thing and that person but I am fine.' You are attempting to interfere with someone else's journey of discovery and it is not your right. Even if they are your child/mother/husband/girlfriend, you have no right to change them. You will do more to prevent them learning because you are providing them with a wall to kick against, giving them an excuse not to change and to stick their heels in. By seeking to impose your ideas of how they should change you are causing the opposite, because they must and will teach you that it does not happen like this. And they have no right to change you unless you yourself choose it.

Support and co-operation

You can of course ask people to work with you, to help you grow. It can be a mutually agreed change. But the desire must still come from within the individual, for their own growth, in their own time and direction. There is an absence of ego in this second scenario. It is with love and not ego that we have agreed to help each other learn and grow, not compulsion, using threats and coercion. If we decide we know how someone ought to be then we are saying that we know better than anyone else, which is arrogant. Who are you to want someone to change, to become what you think they should be? If we do not like the experience of being close to the other person, we should leave them to it and move on for ourselves. Everyone is as they need to be, in order to teach and to learn their lessons. In this way they are perfect and are teaching us to let go of our ideas as being right or wrong, to learn acceptance. Nothing is wrong and we must accept it. Our ego wants to judge and criticise, to be right, and everything out there to be wrong.

Humans have falsely identified themselves with the ego or false self and from this comes all lack and suffering.

When we release our self from ego control and become our true self, our spiritual self, we find there is no suffering. It is all joy and love.

The further down this path we travel, the more we can see this is true. *The voice of fear is the voice of ego*, but it is an illusion and when we look at it with the eyes of truth and trust we can see it is nothing but a shadow in our life.

Summary

This chapter has addressed many points relating to the experiences of our human reality.

- ◆ Your ego is part of you yet not your whole nature.
- ◆ Fighting the ego is fighting yourself, so who can win?
- ◆ Self-knowledge means self-mastery and revealing your true potential.
- ◆ Recognising the strategies of the ego allows you to master it and become response-able.
- ◆ Making a commitment to yourself to overcome all aspects of fear in yourself is making a demonstration of your love for and acceptance of yourself.
- ◆ Loving your real self, your whole self, means that others can love you too.

CHAPTER 5

Dealing with Fear and Anger

F ear is the predominant emotion and motivation of all ego strategies. As discussed in the last chapter the ego has one desire, to protect us. It does this in the best possible way it can, but it does so through the illusions of human experience because it is conscious only of these realities.

> Remember, the ego can easily be recognised as 'earth guide only'.

Fear is the basis of nearly all uncomfortable emotions and experiences. There are two emotional states, there is either a state of joy/love or a state of fear. Everything in our life is an expression or demonstration of our own individual balance between these two influences. All we feel, that seems negative, is a demonstration of some aspect of our fear. It is a sign of our separation from our whole self. The most common variations of fear that prevent us experiencing our true value in life and achieving a life we really want are:

◆ anger
◆ guilt
◆ shame
◆ revenge
◆ jealousy
◆ possessiveness.

Of course there are as many variations of fear as we can find adjectives to describe them (see Figure 7). Exploring the many ways in which emotions are expressed means we can identify them in our selves and release our life from their control and limitations.

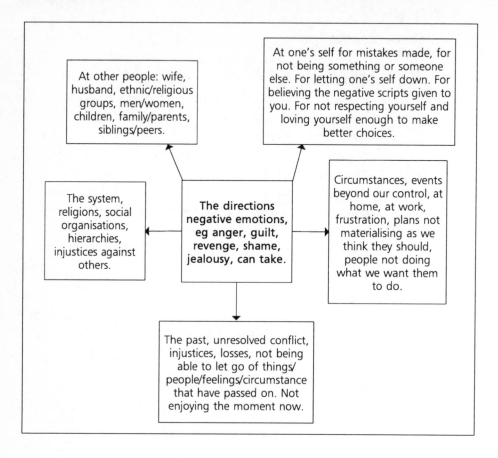

Fig. 7. Negative emotions routes.

Identifying anger

We all experience anger at some stage of our lives. Anger is no more than a reaction to a set of circumstances with which we feel unhappy, and as such is no different to any other emotional response we might feel. The problem with anger is that it is usually damaging, not only to the person who is feeling angry but to the person on the receiving end.

Anger, like any emotion, becomes extremely powerful if it is allowed to build up. It seems to take us in its grip and rush us along into situations we would have preferred not to visit, or to destroy things we would have wanted to keep, especially relationships. Anger is a fear of events or circumstances not going as you think they should, not being in control, not suiting your needs.

Emotional messengers

Anger is not a totally destructive force. Like all emotions it is a flag indicating that 'this is not a good situation'. It is a messenger telling us how we feel about a given set of circumstances. It is information we can use. Anger only damages when we hold on to it. If we see the anger and not the message it is giving us, we are missing the opportunity to understand our choices in life.

We all have choices. By recognising your own sources of anger, you can find alternatives to use instead of anger. These can include:

◆ Choices of response – we can find other ways of responding.

◆ Choices of perception – we can see the situation or the other person in a different light.

◆ Choices of interpretation – we can interpret the situation in a positive way, seeing opportunities.

◆ Choices of circumstance – we can choose to take our self out of a situation and change our life.

Try it now

What does anger represent in your life? You might like to try this with other emotions at some stage too, but for now use anger as a starting point. Look at the following list and see which ones apply to you. Add any others you can think of.

◆ a means of release
◆ a means of attack
◆ a weapon
◆ a form of control
◆ a lack of control
◆ a bargaining tool
◆ a sign of fear
◆ a sign of frustration
◆ a sign of vulnerability
◆ a warning
◆ an expression of one's feelings
◆ a symptom of deeper problems
◆ a release of energy.

Recognising the fear basis of anger is the first step to learning to manage and control it and towards freedom from its tyranny. You might say that we cannot change our basic personality and that some people are angry people. Who we are is not based on what we feel but on how we learn from what happens, how we deal with life. It is based on the choices we make. The fundamental choice we can all make is to change that within ourself which most separates us from the life we want to live.

◆ Would you choose to feel angry if you knew about alternatives?

◆ Does anger make you feel comfortable and content, happy with your lot in life?

◆ Does it leave you feeling exhausted and unsettled?

◆ Does anger leave you wanting to 'do something', to change things your way?

◆ Does it leave you regretting your behaviour but confused about what else you could do?

◆ Does anger leave you feeling out of control?

Once we recognise what it is in our life that makes us feel angry, we can begin to see what we are frightened of. We can recognise our behaviour and decide to change.

Try it now

This is a long exercise but it really allows you to consider your anger at a deep level. Tick each of the following lists, then consider alternatives. As you work through the lists decide, for each one you tick, if this is your preferred choice and if it achieves your intended outcome:

1 *How do you show anger?*

◆ Shouting or swearing, using volume to dominate.

◆ Smouldering silence, glowering, refusing to discuss issues.

◆ Damaging objects, throwing things, punching doors, kicking etc.

◆ Feeling self-pity, taking a victim attitude, transferring blame and guilt, avoiding responsibility.

◆ Becoming depressed, withdrawing, sulking, crying.

◆ Self-harming, eg cutting, or abusing substances/food.

◆ Physically attacking others, losing control physically.

◆ Taunting others, verbally assaulting, winning points.

◆ Criticising others, finding faults that justify your position.

◆ Gesticulating, threatening physical behaviour.

2 *How do you feel when you are angry?*
◆ anxious
◆ out of control
◆ unhappy
◆ aggressive
◆ vengeful
◆ bitter
◆ cruel
◆ frustrated
◆ annoyed
◆ trapped
◆ victimised
◆ hostile
◆ alone
◆ misunderstood
◆ disbelieved
◆ afraid.

3 *What causes you to feel anger?*
◆ Frustration – being ignored, not listened to.
◆ Betrayal – deceived, believing what you are told and not your own instincts.
◆ Being alone and lonely – thinking that other people should consider your needs.
◆ Vulnerability – aware of your reliance on others, uncertainty, challenged by new situations.
◆ Disappointment – promises unfulfilled, others not doing what you think they should.
◆ Physical changes – illness, ageing, disability, geographic or social/material changes.
◆ Confusion – not knowing which way to go or what will happen next.
◆ Being treated badly – insults, accepting abusive treatment, believing low self-worth messages from others.
◆ Being disbelieved – not having your truth or experiences honoured, being denied your feelings.
◆ A feeling of being trapped – by relationships, responsibilities.
◆ Being attacked – verbally, symbolically or physically.

◆ Injustice – your rights being dismissed and over-ridden.

4   *What does anger achieve for you?*

◆ a form of release
◆ shows how strongly you feel about something
◆ shows your vulnerability
◆ acts as a warning sign
◆ damages relationships, causes dispute
◆ damages oneself
◆ causes frustration as well as releasing it
◆ makes you unhappy and unleashes negative energy, makes you stressed
◆ damages a healing process
◆ makes people afraid of you.

Anger can be directed in many ways, but if you explore the above lists you will see that ultimately it is you taking the brunt of your own anger. Whoever it is directed at is only feeling their own emotions and their own agendas, not yours.

Other forms of fear

Guilt, shame, revenge, jealousy and possessiveness are actually quite similar to each other. They come from a single sense – a sense of lack, a fear that we are not good enough or that our needs will not be met.

Guilt

Guilt is a fear of being found out that you are less than perfect or less than you would like to be seen as, that you don't want people to know about. But it is actually more about low self-esteem. It is a lack of self-acceptance, of acceptance of your human fallibility and that you are going to get things wrong from time to time, so you feel guilty.

Shame

Shame is the fear of other people seeing you are not the person you would really like to be. It is the fear of our own self-dislike being recognised by others, being exposed for all that we are.

Guilt is usually internal, shame is external, though other people can make us feel guilty and we can feel ashamed of ourselves without anybody else being involved.

Conflicting senses of self

The difficulty with guilt and shame is that they are based on the idea that:

◆ we really aren't very nice, and have secrets to hide from others

◆ we want to be the nice person and that isn't the truth.

There is the sense of separation from the true self. *The truth is we are all both.* We are human, full of great things and some not very skilful things. But our potential is limitless.

> We are perfect in our imperfections. It is through the interaction of all aspects of each of us that we learn and teach each other.

If we are in conflict with our self about our own value, we are wasting energy we could be using to create a constructive life that we really want. The universal laws of creation, of the power of thoughts to create realities, will not argue back at us. It will not try to convince us we are wrong. It is up to us. Things will continue as they always have until we choose to see that truth for our self. Then we will start to manifest all that we want in life.

Revenge

Revenge is the belief that someone else is responsible for our difficulties and we want to make them pay. It is a desire to make someone else feel guilty or ashamed of themselves. Revenge has voices like:

◆ see what you did to me/my life/my opportunities

◆ see what a mess my life is because of you

◆ see how damaged I am because of what you did

◆ look at how bad my health is because of the trauma you put me through

◆ look at how poor I am because of what happened to me.

Revenge is a very destructive form of self-pity; **poor me**, the voice of the ego ruling our life.

Revenge means we are refusing to take responsibility for our own lives and seeking to make others miserable too. A double trump against our self. The event is over unless we have chosen to remain and allow it to continue, and 'they' are usually long gone. So who are we really hurting? If people such as parents, ex-partners, ex-friends and employers have treated us inappropriately, we have a choice: move away from this situation or change the way we feel about our self and earn their change in behaviour. The only time in our life when this is really not usually possible is in childhood; this is a different issue and too big to explore in depth here. We are not dismissing its importance but this book is aimed at what we can do now, in our adult lives. We have choices. We can choose to move on and begin to let go.

Jealousy

Jealousy is a belief that someone else has something, can do something or be something that you can't. You want to have something that someone else has or be something that someone else is. That is based on the fact that you don't value yourself and who you are, thinking that what this person is or has is better. You are not valuing what you *have* got in your life – and if you don't value it, it does not feel like a good thing to have.

Possessiveness

Possessiveness is a belief that what you have will be lost to you if you don't guard it carefully. You somehow have to control it in order to hang on to it. It comes from a belief in lack and limitation. It denies the idea that any 'loss' always results in a gain somewhere else.

Digging for the causes

All negative emotions are based on the fear that:
◆ We either have or are less than we need or want to be.
◆ We are less than we really are, our own self-belief is

undervaluing our true nature.

◆ If we lack something, it's the result of some injustice or unfairness in life.

◆ If something goes missing in life a vacuum will be created.

◆ Our needs will not be met and we must fight to protect our needs and rights.

If we take the concept of thought creates reality, or the self-fulfilling prophesy, and we hold beliefs like the ones listed above, what will our experience be in life? And if we believe that our experience is the whole truth, we are well and truly stuck in those experiences. But the reality is different if and when you allow it to be. The truth is we can't have vacuums in our lives, because if something leaves then something will come to take its place. This means releasing the loss from our emotions, in order to make room for new feelings and experiences.

Our fears are our creations

All fears are based on an illusion that we create. Because we create it, we believe it, and because we believe it, it becomes a reality. But illusions are like shadows. People who come into our lives and make us uncomfortable are our **shadow selves**.

◆ They mirror back to us that which we do not like in ourselves.

◆ They mirror back to us our belief in fear, and the power and control it has over us.

◆ They show us that which we fear or dislike in ourselves.

When we recognise them for what they really are, an illusion, we can start to accept the teaching and eradicate the cause of our fear. We can also love the person even if we do not like their behaviour. We can accept their teaching. These themes will be developed in greater depth later.

Solutions

Whatever has happened up until the moment you read this sentence is in the past, and you cannot change that. But at this precise moment, now, you can make the decision to change the future for yourself. Every single moment is another opportunity for you to change and to transform your reality, to begin creating the life you want to live.

All the spiritual psychological teachings tell us that all our needs are met all the time. That is difficult to accept at first because sometimes it feels as though they are not being met. The reason they appear not to be met is because we are *not* thinking 'right here, right now, all our needs are met'. We are thinking:

♦ in the next half hour, or in the next week, or in the next month they may not be met

♦ last week things didn't work out as I wanted them to or thought they should do.

So we are projecting either forwards or back and that is where the difficulty is coming from. We are hanging on to old stuff or we are creating stuff that hasn't even happened yet. Everything is fine in the moment when we recognise that.

Positive 'revenge'

If we really believe that someone wants to hurt us, then surely the best revenge we can have is to *not* be hurt, to be happy irrespective of them. This demonstrates their lack of power over us.

♦ They have not succeeded even if it was their conscious intent that we should be damaged or hurt.

♦ They are insignificant in the greater view of our life, a mere blip in our potential unfolding.

♦ They are actually providing us with an excellent example of what not to do in life.

We address concepts of skilful choices and recipes for living in the appendices. These are guidelines from which we can construct our individual approach and choices in life that will bring nothing but positive manifestation in return. Being a victim, being angry or full of revenge, being ashamed and jealous, only hurts us. It cannot hurt our persecutors. So who is hurting whom? The truth is we do it to ourselves.

Recognising our position in the monkey trap

The lesson to be learned is that of 'letting go'. To explain this in simple terms it is useful to refer to what is known as the monkey trap. In the rainforests of South America some tribes carve out the inside of gourds, leaving a hole in the top just big enough for a monkey to slip its open hand into. Inside the gourd they place some fruit or nuts. Then they tie the gourd to the ground and leave it. Sooner or later the monkey comes along, and smelling the food inside the gourd, slips its hand in through the hole in the top and grabs the food. Unfortunately for the monkey, the hole in the gourd is not big enough for a clenched fist to exit. The monkey is trapped. Either it lets go of the food, or it escapes. Logic tells us that they should let go of the food, but this is not what happens. Despite being trapped it refuses to let go of what it thinks it wants. Even when the hunters return and it sees them coming to kill, they will not let go. The trap has worked.

Self-destruct tendencies

Just as the monkey refuses to let go of the food and is destroyed by its own action, so it is with those who allow themselves to hold on to the feelings which create long-term anger etc. There is a self-destructive refusal to accept their part in their own misery. No one else can open the hand that holds on so desperately to the past. It is as if letting go means loss.

Why do people want to hold on to the things which hurt them? There are several reasons.

◆ They think that if they let go there will be nothing else to fill the void. This of course is untrue. Just as the food in the gourd is only a tiny amount of food in the forest so the world is full of opportunity and possibility. If you don't let go, then how can there be room for anything else to come into your life?

◆ Some people see letting go as 'giving in', an admission perhaps that they had something to do with the problems which are at the root of their anger. As no one in the world is perfect, of course they had something to do with what happened. Again, letting go allows the other person or persons off the hook. What hook? Think again, who is the one who's hooked? Who is the one that's trapped? Who is hurting?

The more one looks at long-term anger and other negative beliefs and emotions, the more it becomes recognisable as self-inflicted. Only by individuals understanding themselves and taking the time and effort to explore their own feelings can their anger finally heal. This healing then leads you on to a universe of opportunities for creating a life you want to live.

Learning to trust

We deal with this in greater depth in the next couple of chapters but here it is important to make a few points.

All the teaching says that if we learn to trust and let go of all our fears then all our needs will be met and we can actually experience life in its fullness. Now who is going to meet our needs? It isn't anything out there. Everything starts from within. It is this lack of trust that maintains the idea that our needs won't be met next week, they are not met now and they weren't met in the past. One difficulty is: what are your needs?

Mirrors of reality

We come back to the idea of mirroring; that everything out there is a mirror of what is going on inside you. To improve your life, what you most need to know is *what you need to recognise about yourself next, what you need to learn in order to move on in your life*. Your needs:

◆ may not be to have a nice easy comfortable life
◆ may not be to have millions of pounds coming your way easily
◆ may be to learn that you don't need those in order to be happy
◆ may be to give you challenges to bring your strengths out
◆ may be to test your resolve and depth of trust as fully unconditional.

Differentiating needs and wants

A testing situation may be your need, but we perceive it as a difficulty, as something we don't want. Our perception is 'there is something bad happening here'. That is the difficulty, because it is the belief in two powers: in good and bad, right and wrong. So we need to think about whether this *is* actually a bad experience, or if we can learn something from it.

If we are faced with a situation that makes us

- ◆ feel insecure and uncertain
- ◆ brings out our feelings of guilt, shame, anger, possessiveness or jealousy

then what we are being shown is that:

- ◆ we don't need those feelings,
- ◆ but we do have them inside us
- ◆ and that is why we need to get rid of them.

It is as difficult as we make it, or rather as our ego makes it for us. We all need to realise that these are ideals. We will all get there eventually, there is no rush and we have to be compassionate with who we are now.

> When we realise where we could be heading, it makes it easier to move from where we are now. It doesn't mean that we are going to get from 'here' to 'there' in one go. It is a step.

Some people can make that quantum leap in terms of consciousness. Most of us have to work at it, layer by layer. It can feel a bit like wading through treacle or mud until we eventually free ourself. So the more you pull yourself out of these negative beliefs you hold, the faster you start being able to move, but also the deeper you have to go into yourself. It starts becoming easier when you recognise immediately what you are being shown and what you can do to heal yourself and move on more quickly.

Recognising goals

All aspects of fear result in us withholding a full realisation of who we are. If we are caught up in negative emotions they block us off. They prevent us from expressing our full potential, with all the love and compassion that we actually have. All of us are loving, compassionate people. It's just that things make us feel 'I am not going to love there' or 'I'm not going to feel compassionate there'.

We close ourselves off because we believe we need to protect ourselves. But wouldn't you say we all desire to be loving and compassionate to everybody, and for everybody to have the same response to us? Having all your needs met without fear or anxiety is a lovely goal to go towards. You might hear others suggest it is completely unrealistic to think that anyone can ever get there. But we prefer to think that it's unrealistic to think that we won't all get there, and what is wrong with aspiring?

> Remember belief creates reality.

Some people have already achieved this goal and for others it seems an impossibility; what is the difference in the beliefs of these people? Being angry and demanding that others recognise our worth is useless and pointless until we can lovingly know our own worth and live it.

Accepting the whole self

We are denying ourselves access to our own self-acceptance. Our love of our whole self, not just aspects of ourself, is total self-acceptance.

◆ It is an acceptance of all things we do, or do not do, that may have questionable aspects to them.

◆ It is accepting that we all have qualities that have to be dealt with in different ways, without judgement or condemnation.

◆ It is moving away from the fears that we are less than adequate, that we cannot meet our own needs.

The fact that you are reading this book now means that, up until now, you have actually coped with everything life has sent. It might have felt like you weren't going to but actually you always have, haven't you? Otherwise you wouldn't be here right now. Consider:

◆ who is meeting your needs

- ◆ who has always met your needs
- ◆ who will always be able to meet your needs

but you?

Do you completely trust that whatever situation comes up you will be able to survive it and deal with it and move on from it? Or do you feel 'I don't want this to happen, I won't be able to cope with that. Help...'?

Avoiding fear-based judgements

We are scared of our belief that we are inadequate. The truth is we are *more than adequate* to cope with all that life can throw at us. We have always coped until now, but we believe that we haven't because we think that we should have done it differently or better, or somehow it shouldn't have happened. These are the illusory beliefs that teach us to fear what might happen next. Out of these illusory beliefs we feel:

- ◆ Ashamed or guilty for what has happened in the past.
- ◆ Fearful and angry about what has been done to us.
- ◆ Jealous that this person coped and we didn't.
- ◆ We want revenge on someone who has mirrored back to us that which we refuse to accept.

Making choices

We can make judgements based on an understanding of the choices which bring our preferred outcome; it is a discernment. It is not saying 'this is right or wrong', it is merely saying 'this is the best way I can behave to get what I really want'. It is about being true to ourselves and not giving our self anything to feel fearful about later. If we deny our inappropriate choices, we cannot accept our lessons and move on from them. It keeps us trapped in a life we do not want, but that we create for ourselves.

Summary

Your thoughts create your reality. Keep this principle in mind, and know that it is a principle. It applies whether we like it or not. Then you can start to recognise how you create your present situation and how you can change it.

- ◆ Change always starts with recognising what you really believe.
- ◆ Beliefs are formed in many layers and what you think you believe may not be the full story.
- ◆ Negative beliefs are based on fears and block you from your true value.
- ◆ Accepting responsibility for your life is a central step in accepting your potential to change.
- ◆ The value you place on your self will be mirrored back in all aspects of your life.

CHAPTER 6

Recognising Your Illusions

When we speak of illusion, in the context of human existence, we are not talking about the conjuring tricks performed by some amateur magician, or the mirage seen across the burning desert by a sun-parched traveller. Illusion is far more than either a trick or misapprehension. Illusion is *incorrect perception* due to lack of understanding; failure to see what it is that makes us what we are, and failure, having understood this, to act upon such knowledge. The dictionary defines illusion as 'something a person wrongly supposes to exist, or a false belief about the nature of something'. So what are the things we humans might wrongly suppose to exist, what false beliefs might we have?

Understanding the power of subjective experience

Let us start with the birth of a child. What beliefs does that child have? What beliefs can you recall having when you were a month old, or 18 months old? It would be surprising if you answered that you had any. It is in later life that we begin to create opinions about, and concepts of, what we call reality. For the newly born child life is as it comes, fluid, timeless, accepted as experience and nothing more.

As we grow up, we start forming mental patterns called **structures** or **schemas**. These create our personal view of reality. Gradually we learn the lessons of life, and are taught to behave in particular ways, both by observation and direct teaching. Then the fluid and intuitive behaviour becomes rigid and restrictive. We learn:

◆ who we are, according to other people's perceptions
◆ how to relate to other people, according to social rules
◆ what is expected of us
◆ what we can expect
◆ what the world about us is, and is not, based on cultural and social norms.

A child is given a whole host of concepts and rules by which they are expected to live their lives. These, more often than not, have been handed down from generation to generation: forms of behaviour, systems of belief, attitudes of mind. This process is called **socialisation**, and enables each individual to fit into the family, and then the greater society in which they are born.

Taught realities

Reality is based upon numerous conceptual ideas not necessarily held in common globally. Into these an individual invests their belief in themselves and life generally. One only has to think of religious belief to understand how many forms of that particular reality there are. Each believer will hold out that their God is the real God, their way is the right way, and of course to them this is the truth. Most religious structures teach that their spiritual beliefs are 'the truth', and most humanistic and scientific explanations to life will state their claim equally.

A number of ideas combine together to create 'reality'. Like religious belief, a number of other beliefs are fundamentally held on trust. Someone holding strong religious views may say 'it's not trust, we have the Bible' or 'we have the Koran'. The word trust is used in this context on the basis that the miraculous events portrayed in any religious writings have seldom been proved empirically. Assumptions have been made about the plagues of Egypt, for example, which show that they probably did happen and might be explained scientifically but no one can actually *prove* it to be so.

Try it now   Think of some of the beliefs you hold. Ask yourself whether you have ever had cause to prove them to someone else. How much have you questioned these beliefs? How open are you to hearing opposing beliefs and considering them with equal respect?

We either accept what we are told by others, or weigh up the alternatives and work on what feels comfortable, without questioning this process. We need to become fully aware of exactly those processes in our self.

Proof and evidence

Most of us would have a hard job proving just how far away
the Sun is from the Earth. If you were told it was 93 million
miles away, you might readily accept this to be true because it
sounds reasonable, but without going to several authorities on
the subject there's no way you could be sure. It is in fact the
accepted distance, but the point is that even scientific data is
held on trust. We accept what we are told because we have no
way of checking things out for ourselves. We can only accept
the evidence we are given and trust it is so.

Experience and trust

Experience shows that absolute trust in scientific evidence is a
mistake. In England in recent years, salmonella was found in
eggs when government scientists maintained there was no
problem with contamination. More recently there has been the
BSE in beef problem which again, according to government
scientists, did not exist. If we had been born at another time in
history we could have been persecuted for believing that the
Earth was not at the centre of the universe, or locked away as
being mad for thinking that men could leave the planet.

Reality, in a scientific sense, is the point at which current
research has proved to the majority of scientists in any chosen
field that something conforms to a certain rule or pattern and
can be shown to do so repeatedly. Yet a great deal of current
science is theoretical. Particle physics in particular has to be
theoretical for we do not have the tools with which to prove
what is assumed. So once again we have to trust, to believe
without absolute proof.

Illusion and control

Totalitarian states and communities are good examples of
illusion and the desire to believe in something we are told
rather than face the reality of a situation. After the war between
the Communists and the armies of Chang Kai Shek in China,
the country came under the rule of the Communists. Mao Tse
Tung decided that in order to keep control, he would isolate
the country from the rest of the world. He successfully

controlled the media and passage into and out of China.

At first the Communist rule was a welcome change from difficulties of pre-Communist days and the people felt optimistic. But Mao was desperate to show the West that he was achieving greater things than capitalist countries. To prove this, he decided one priority was to produce iron for the foundries. He got the people to smelt cooking utensils, together with any other metal objects they could find. In doing this they used valuable fuel to heat the smelting kilns, spent most of their time looking unproductively for firewood, and produced extremely low grade iron which subsequently caused problems for the manufacturers who used it.

Mao was proud to show that production figures had soared, the people believed in Mao and saw their endeavours as successful. Visitors from the West marvelled at what was happening. But this so-called success was ultimately an illusion. In this case, millions of people believed something they wanted to believe, that Mao Tse Tung could achieve anything he wanted to. They believed what they wanted to believe, and what they wanted to believe became their reality. The reality Mao wanted to create was based on deceit and manipulation, not on trust and the best outcome for everyone. These forms of reality are short lived because they are based on dishonest intent, on ego beliefs and desires.

Similar examples of the 'total institution' phenomenon have been studied by psychologists. The findings show:

◆ isolation and inability to see beyond what they were told
◆ fear of consequences of questioning the official line
◆ no access to alternative terms of reference
◆ rejection of another point of view as a fear reaction.

This means the illusions have the right ingredients to become a reality for a short time. An open and enquiring mind, the freedom to ask questions and access to a range of information and knowledge are the crucial ingredients to being able to choose one's own truth and to avoid being fed an illusory reality.

Accepting our own vulnerability

How consciously aware are you of what you believe in? Are you too sophisticated to believe what you are told without question? Think again:

◆ Have you actively looked at an advertisement?
◆ Have you bought designer label clothing?
◆ Have you changed your colour schemes to match those in vogue?
◆ Have you bought something in a package twice the size needed for the product?
◆ Have you bought something you did not know you needed until you saw the advert and thought you needed it?

Advertising and manufacturing industry have created a ` ` world which we accept into our lives. A reality in whicn.

◆ thin people are happy
◆ old people don't exist
◆ ownership means success
◆ happiness depends on the beer you drink
◆ cars improve personal relationships
◆ achievement is status
◆ being normal means conforming, not being yourself.

No matter how independently minded you think you are, if you live and conform to this model of life you are a part of this particular illusion.

Influences on reality

Religion, science, politics and consumerism are four areas where 'reality' is difficult to pin down. Has this triggered some thoughts about how you might be affected in your daily life by things you hold as true? What about the media? We've looked briefly at advertising, but just as influential is the effect on us of television, radio, films, the press and now the Internet.

Consider this

Do you read a newspaper? Which paper do you read? Does it basically reflect your views on the world? Now think of a list of newspapers and note their political leanings. Some reflect the views of the left in politics, some the right, and others include mainly sport and scandal. We like to look at newspapers because they reflect a certain reality, but it is by no means an objective reality. People don't only read newspapers to be informed, they also read them to obtain confirmation that their view of the world is the correct one.

◆ I am a student so I read a newspaper that tells me all right-wingers are wrong.

◆ I am a right-winger, I read a newspaper that tells me all students are lazy communists.

Although this summary is simplistic, it is the principle which is important. Any one story in a newspaper can be told several ways according to the subjective views of the journalist and editor. Any evidence can be presented to create a desired reality for a period of time. Nothing is permanent.

Media influences on reality

Even more disturbing is the subtle way in which attitudes are manipulated by what we see on the television or films. It used to be called propaganda but nowadays it comes under the banner of public information. Ideas about social issues are fed into programmes and worked into scripts. As a result the public's perception of issues is changed. It may well be for the supposed benefit of information dissemination, but who is to say from which perspective it is written? Remember the newspapers? Whose reality is this?

Illusions of permanence

Having briefly looked at some of the problems with objectively finding reality in the external world, it is time to look again at impermanence and its implications. Most dissatisfaction stems from our desire to believe in the permanence of impermanent things. We cling to ideas, beliefs and objects on the basis that if we let go we will somehow disintegrate, or become lost.

Change, progress and illusion

Fifty years ago it was normal for someone to enter a specific field of work when they left school, and for them to leave work at 65 having stayed in the same business. There was a relative permanence in working lives no matter which end of the scale one started. On the whole coalminers stayed coalminers, doctors stayed doctors, bank employees stayed bank employees. Nowadays this is not so. In Japan thousands of people a year are committing suicide as a result of the shame of losing a job. The attachment to or belief in the security of a particular job is one of the strongest attachments in everyday life and causes devastating consequences when job loss occurs. The loss of a job represents a whole structure of reality:

- loss of income
- loss of status
- loss of purpose
- loss of self-esteem
- loss of the constructed future the individual has, ie promotion.

Once this imagined future disappears they are left floundering. 'Reality isn't as it should be, what am I supposed to do?'

Permanent senses of self

Have you ever taken out an old photograph of yourself and laughed? 'Look at my hair. What did I think I looked like, and those clothes!' We have probably all done this. When you look at an old photograph, who is it that you see? It's you, but then it's not you. It's someone you have been, whose clothes you wouldn't want to wear, or whose clothes you wish you were still able to wear! Nothing stays the same, everything changes, but unfortunately we try to avoid this happening and in so doing become unhappy. The illusion we try to create is one of permanence, and clinging to this false sense of permanence causes us distress.

Try it now   Take an old photograph of yourself and look at it for a moment.

- Can you remember how you felt at that age?

◆ Can you recall what things were important to you at that time?

◆ Can you think of anything that you really desired, really craved for?

◆ If you can recall, those feelings were probably so strong at the time that they temporarily took over your life. How important are they now? Where are the objects of your desire now?

You may look back at the photograph and yearn to be the young carefree person you were, the one without any wrinkles or grey hair, or still want to posses the things you desired years ago. If so you are not living in the present. If these thoughts are always in your mind, you will find it hard to be happy.

Adjusting to impermanence

Although things change constantly, they move at different rates. The Sun is a mass of burning gases which loses thousands of tons of fuel every second, but to us it is permanent. It won't change appreciably for many millions of years to come and as such can be relied upon to rise every morning and set every evening, during our lifetimes, and those of our children and grandchildren. Even though it seems you turn around and suddenly you have a head of grey hair, this isn't the case. The change is relatively slow. We do have a chance to come to terms with it happening. Children grow. Adults look back and say 'where did that time go?' Yet we can sit in a waiting room and think that eternity is passing by. There are degrees of 'temporary'.

Focusing on the present

Many people are unaware of the present. They live their lives in the past, or they live them in the future. What has been, and what is to come, is more important than what is, now.

◆ Why is this so?

◆ What effect does this have upon the quality of life?

Clinging to something which has gone is living an illusion. It is wasting the opportunity to live, now. You can never recapture the past because you are trying to hold on to something which has changed, something which may have been wonderful but which has had its moment. This isn't to say that one shouldn't look back occasionally and recall happy moments. What we are talking about here is the attitude which says:

◆ It was so much better then, when I compare it with now, and as a result I don't want to live in the present.

◆ Nothing will compare to those times, so why bother?

If that is how you think, that is exactly how it will be. We have to learn to let go of the past, to appreciate the good times but to know that *now* holds its own opportunities.

Living in 'what might be'

We all look forward to holidays, to next week's episode of our favourite television programme, to winning the lottery. Sometimes anticipation of an event is just as satisfying as the event itself. Where these attitudes become a problem is when they block out the present, when they are used to compensate for something unsatisfactory in our lives. Once again, like those who live in the past, future-dwellers do not appreciate what they have in the present.

◆ Wouldn't you like to enjoy every moment of your life, and not just the 'special' ones?

◆ Wouldn't you like to wake up every morning and no matter what you had to do, to be able to think, 'I am glad to be awake at this moment'?

Living in peaceful solitude

There is a story about the Buddha who was visiting the court of a wealthy monarch. When the monarch asked the Buddha what he thought he could offer him that he didn't already have the Buddha replied 'how long could you sit at peace and in total contentment? One hour or two?' The monarch felt he could quite easily do this, after all he had wonderful vistas to look at, possessions to count, books to read. The Buddha then said 'a day or two?' The monarch thought for a while and wasn't quite so sure he could manage that. Then the Buddha said 'a week or two?' It was then that the monarch conceded he could not, and he began to see the point the Buddha was making. If you become in tune with now, with the immediate, and learn to live in the present, you can take every moment as a new experience, every moment as a gift not to be overlooked.

Try it now   Think of the last time you were really ill. How did that feel? Now that you are not ill do you ever think of how well you feel? Most people don't. They take for granted the fact that they don't have a splitting headache, or a broken limb, or are just recovering from an operation. Stop now and think of your body. Is it in pain? Hopefully it is not, and if not, do you really appreciate that fact? Do you take the time to notice on a day-to-day basis? There may be someone reading this book who is suffering. Try thinking of them and offer them a positive thought. To those who are in pain just take this thought, that somewhere someone is thinking of you and wishing you well, and that contrary to how it feels at the moment nothing is permanent.

Be aware of your body, take time to think about the positive things – eating, breathing, moving.

Living eternally

If you care to make the effort to live in the present you will find that each day, each moment of the day can be appreciated. Just think about:

◆ how worried we all are about life slipping away
◆ how often we say we have so little time
◆ how we worry about old age and not being able to enjoy ourselves.

Yet what do we do with our time? We spend it:

◆ worrying about the past
◆ planning the future
◆ ignoring the present.

This illusion serves to keep us in a very superficial and totally unsatisfactory world. Repeat the question the Buddha asked, 'how long could you sit at peace and in total contentment?'

Consider the present. Where did it begin – or end? The immediate now is never ending. It flows along eternally.

Keeping in the present

As mindfulness develops, time takes on a different aspect. What happened yesterday or what is going to happen tomorrow become less important, you actually begin to live your life, to feel it rather than thinking it. Regrets you have, or fears you may have about what is to come, are put in their place.

◆ Why waste days or weeks thinking ahead about exams, projects, forming all sorts of agonising scenarios when you don't have to?

◆ Why spend nights desperately churning over the same old history when you could be at peace, knowing that now is what matters?

Children know how to be mindful. When a small child builds a sandcastle, when they paint or draw, when they play a game, they are totally absorbed in the present. Parents call to them and they don't hear, time is not relevant. At this point you may well be saying 'that's all very well, children don't have to earn a living, and look after the household'. This is true, but they have not yet lost the art of mindfulness. You can earn a living, run a household, be a committee member, garden, write letters etc and still be mindful.

> Learn to look and feel, to be a part of your surroundings wherever they may be.

Come off autopilot and be alive.

Thinking beyond illusion

To think beyond illusion, one has to turn to the teachings of any of the mystical traditions. They all say the same thing ultimately, and all struggle to find a way of putting it into words. This is where the difficulty with illusion deepens. It is more of an experience, a feeling one has after thinking along these lines for some time and after exploring your own quietness inside through meditation, contemplation or prayer. We have chosen a mystical form of Buddhism, Zen.

What is Zen Buddhism?

Zen is one of many schools of Buddhism, but unlike any other it is prepared to disregard the Buddha and all of his teachings. So how can you have a school of philosophy which strives to eradicate the very teacher and teachings which led it into existence? That is the nature of Zen. In modern terms it is minimalist in its approach. It has no regard for ritual, for repetition, for the sanctity of teachings or of the enlightenment of the Buddha.

What then is Zen? To answer this question is not to answer it, according to those who know Zen. If it can be described, then it is not Zen. For Zen is such a difficult and yet such a simple concept, that to try to explain it would seem madness and to walk away would make much more sense. A glimpse is all anyone can offer, for Zen is like the flash of a fish in a pond, no sooner have you glimpsed it than it has gone: did you really see it?

> The aim of all mystical teaching such as Zen is to touch the inner core of our being as simply as possible. Yet the simplicity is the hardest part for us because we surround it with explanation.

The nature of words

The one substantial thing about Zen is the way it is transmitted from master to student. This is often via mind-wrenching statements or questions called *koans*. You may have heard of some of the better known ones such as:

♦ What is the sound of one hand clapping?
♦ If the flag moves is it the flag or the wind?
♦ Does a falling tree in a forest make a noise if there is no one there to hear it?

You may also have heard of actions by masters and students

which defy reason, such as the master who asked the student what his pointing stick was, at which the student took it from him and breaking it in two said 'what is this?'

Searching for meaning

What possible meaning can such things have? Is there some hidden code which only adepts of Zen can grasp after years of contemplation? It is to the nature of words we must look for an explanation of that which cannot be explained. We use words to:

♦ describe
♦ communicate
♦ remember
♦ plan.

We may do a number of other things, but let's just stay with these four things for the time being.

Structures, words and beliefs

The world is constructed using words as reference points. The external world has a physical existence. In order to describe and retain it we use words. This means it has an internal, language based existence too. We take the world in through one or other of our senses, and we catalogue it. Now here we have a definite link to the ideas of the Buddha. *Dhukka* (the dissatisfaction caused by impermanence), otherwise called suffering, in part comes from the fact that we are physical beings experiencing through our senses.

Returning to this catalogue of things, what is it like? It's rather like one of those splendid molecule models biologists use to explain how life is constructed. An example of this idea is shown in Figure 8 where a number of words are accessed by a key word. In the example we have the name of a dog called Barney which is the tag with which his owners remember their pet. Barney has a number of attributes and he becomes Barney, the black labrador with brown eyes, a faithful friend who is there when the owner gets home from work and a companion on walks.

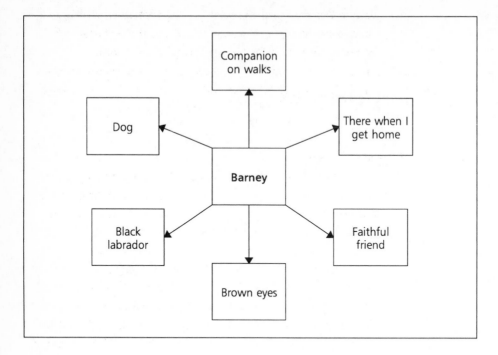

Fig. 8. Constructing a framework.

Because we are programmed to construct frameworks from words, Barney becomes a trigger to a thousand and one other words. Not only this, but the words are, in most cases, linked to emotional recollections, or feeling memories. Barney has two existences, one in the physical world and the other in the mind or minds of his owners. Barney of course doesn't know this, he just 'is'.

◆ Wipe out the memories which Barney's owners have of Barney, and Barney would still exist somewhere in time.

◆ Wipe out Barney, and his owners would still have their memories, their internalised creation of Barney.

Both versions of Barney exist but become largely independent of each other. Rather like a shadow, our internalised world depends on something solid to enable it to exist, and like a shadow it never exactly represents the object of which it is a reflection. It is always distorted and constantly changing.

The example of Barney illustrates what is essentially a one-way transaction. Barney does what Barney does and it is therefore fairly straightforward to construct an appropriate shadow. However, when we start to look at the interaction between human beings the process takes on another dimension. You talk to a shadow person, who talks to you – a similar distortion in their minds – whilst you have your own image of yourself and they have one of themselves.

Social agreements of reality

For social contact to continue, we make unspoken agreements to accept certain 'truths' or rules about the world around us. Barney only needs to exist physically for us to relate to him, but as human beings we need to give and exchange information for our complex relationships to work.

An appropriate example would be our acceptance that time exists and that we are prepared to abide by the rules of the 24-hour clock. If we unilaterally decided to make our day 22 hours long, with 70-minute hours, what would happen? The appointments we made would be a shambles. When we turned on the television to watch a programme it would already have happened. We would always be late for work, and there would never be midnight. When someone's mind is damaged, say by disease, we clearly see the results of failure to abide by the rules, or rather, failure to understand them any more. They lose the ability to retain the standard, internalised world and see another world, just as real. We will return to this at a later stage in our consideration of Zen.

Frameworks of meaning

Take the idea of frameworks further, and consider if our whole lives are structured around these frameworks. Just as Barney is a distinct framework (a number of words linked to emotional states and recollections), so are you and I, and the things in which we believe. Other concepts we construct, and agree to accept in our everyday lives are:

◆ time
◆ ownership
◆ individual identity
◆ religious deities

◆ truth
◆ morality
◆ archetypes.

One could fill books with concepts, but to give the impression
that our minds are full of distinct, individual frameworks all
functioning in isolation would be misleading. Having accepted
that these frameworks exist, we can recognise that they can be
inter-linked when necessary. Those familiar with computer
programming will know that if you want to repeat a set of
instructions you create a sub-routine, and these sub-routines
can be placed in libraries. For example the instructions 'take
what you see on screen, and send it to the printer, using the
coloured ink cartridge to print' do not need to be constantly
rewritten. You just type out these instructions in programming
language and then you place these in a library under the
heading 'print'. Similarly certain frameworks have links to
other frameworks using key words, key emotions or by the
urgency they contain. Some frameworks are accessed only when
the brain signals a certain level of activity, perhaps firing a
certain number of times at a particular synapse.

Recognising personal creations of reality

From this you can see how we create a sense of reality. Let's go
back to Barney. He starts to whine, his owner wonders why.
Already the owner has accessed 'Barney' and from a branch on
the framework he accesses 'behaviour'. Behaviour has a link to
another framework called 'Barney's behaviour'. In this are listed
all of the things that Barney has been known to do over the
years. From this framework there is a branch called whining.
This links to a framework called 'whining' which contains a list
of reasons as to why Barney might whine. A branch on this tree
says 'if it's after 6 in the evening he probably wants to go for a
walk'. There are three points to make here:

1 The general process described above is what is called logic,
   ie, the process of accessing information, determining what
   that information means, and taking a decision as to how
   you want to respond, if at all.

2   Logic relies upon language, which is based on words which are symbols representing one or a number of things.

3   Frameworks constructed of words not only give us information, they trigger responses too. It would be of no use at all if, having heard Barney and then accessed information about the reason he was whining, his owner sat down, had a cup of tea and totally ignored him. Somewhere on the return journey from 'if it's after 6 he probably wants to go for a walk' a response is triggered, perhaps from a multiple choice framework which says 'if I don't he will continue to annoy me', 'if I don't he will pee on the carpet', 'if I don't the chances are my wife will take him' and so on.

Usually the whole process is instantaneous, and Barney's owner doesn't even know why he took the decision he finally arrived at. There could of course have been external factors such as it was raining, or it wasn't 'his turn', or he wasn't feeling well, which impacted on his choice. Once again the list is endless, but it is the principle we need to grasp. One's personal reality is created using frameworks and these frameworks rely upon words.

A question of time

Science tells us that time exists. We experience time in one form or another and we can, within limits, measure it. However, unlike Barney it can't be seen. We reference it by using agreed parameters. Each day contains 24 hours, each hour 60 minutes and once a year, unlike our neighbours, we put the clocks forward in the spring and back in the autumn. Such is clock time. Fairly easy to understand once you have learnt the rules and agree to abide by them.

What about the future? Where is it? How do we know it's waiting to arrive? We trust this, based on the premise that what has happened before will happen again, ie frameworks. If it wasn't for words constructing frameworks we wouldn't be able to have any concept of time. Think about it – what is the future?

◆ It is something that *might* happen.

- Once it is here it immediately becomes something else, called the present or the past.
- It has no substance.
- It cannot be seen.
- It can be infinite or momentary.

Animals don't plan ahead. They can't construct the future in their mind, because they have no words with which to do so.

Abstract thinking

Abstract thinking is constructing the possibility of something that may or may not happen. Barney's owner did this when they had the choice of leaving Barney, whilst hoping that someone else would take Barney for a walk.

It is important to understand abstract thinking because most of our day-to-day decisions contain degrees of it. Take crossing a road for example. If you make it a rule never to cross the road unless the road is empty to avoid getting run over, then you may die of old age before you manage to cross. Most people use their powers of abstract thinking to assess the state of the traffic, whether they feel their legs can carry them across quickly enough, and on that basis when it is the right time to cross. They have projected the future in order to make a decision.

The question of God and the unicorn

We've looked at structures based on physical things such as Barney. So-called 'real time' can be measured. Time past leaves traces of itself in the form of artefacts, memory, written information, etc. So even though it is not tangible in itself, its impact on the physical world is such that the construction of frameworks to cope with it is not difficult.

However, when we come to a concept such as the existence of God we have more of a problem. What do we have to hang on our framework? Like time, most of us can't see God. God has existed forever. Nothing existed before God. God is perfect, and created everything, is everything. Belief in God cannot rest on empirical evidence. By believing in God you:

- have reached a branch on a framework which doesn't actually touch another one
- give yourself a choice and do what you did with future time
- assume you can rely upon certain things as being true, despite the fact there is nothing at the end of this framework to back it up
- take a leap of faith, and that leap of faith is actually a leap from one framework to a disconnected framework called, for the sake of argument, 'belief'.

Now this framework called 'belief' has never been used before in this way. Whereas the framework called 'doubt' was full of negatives and words/statements of distrust, 'belief' is full of positives such as 'joy' 'optimism' 'compassion' 'expectation', and as a result you feel elated and 'full of the holy spirit'. Now God, like the unicorn, really does exist – ask any Western child to paint God and they can. God has a long white beard, long flowing robes and sits on a cloud, but there is more than this: God exists *because he is allowed to exist*, just like the unicorn.

Deconstructing the structures

What is it that the Zen master can teach the student? Does he really give him the key to the universe in a phrase? In a sense he does because he unlocks the fixed way that the student thinks about the universe and in so doing allows him access to unfettered thought.

As yet no one knows precisely how thinking happens, but it is examination of the principle that matters and not the process. We have seen that:

- frameworks contain information
- frameworks are word or language based
- frameworks have trigger points which allow them to be used
- some of these frameworks have an element of emotion attached to them
- this emotional weighting affects the way in which thought processes progress beyond any particular framework.

For example, someone who has knowledge of the effects of fire upon flesh, ie pain, when confronted by fire avoids contact with it. The emotional trauma of getting burned, attached to the 'fire' framework, strongly says 'back off, don't look for another option'. We all have this embedded in us because at some stage in our lives we have all experienced being burnt.

Patterns and frameworks

These frameworks are very useful for the lives we lead, even essential. You wouldn't get out of bed in the morning unless you had a concept of time, linked to the desire to eat breakfast. They are so good at what they do, most people don't even know they exist, and certainly don't think about them. They are like the autonomic nervous system which keeps the body ticking over. We don't have to think about keeping our heart going, or digesting food or breathing. Our reliance upon these frameworks and the fact that they can come to a decision for us means that for the most part we don't make decisions, they are made automatically. This speeds up decision-making and leads to consistency of approach. The mind says, 'I've done this before, this is how I should react/behave'.

Over the years, as we grow we develop a personality, the 'I' that we think we are.

◆ I believe in this
◆ I don't like that
◆ I am afraid of such and such.

We gather together these frameworks without being aware of them, and they combine to form the person we perceive ourselves to be. To the individual, their sense of 'I' is the ultimate reality. What greater truth can there be than that?

The paradox

There is a paradox with frameworks. By using them to speed up decision-making they necessarily limit it at the same time. You will more often than not think the same way every time you come across the same problem. In Buddhist terms this is holding on, and this is our first real glimpse of the fish in the

pond. When the Zen master asks what his pointing stick
is, the unenlightened will refer to the frameworks and say 'it is
a stick, what else can it be?' This of course is the wrong reply,
and only serves to prove that they have missed the point.
Frameworks:

◆ inhibit free thinking
◆ load us down with the weight of emotion attached to them.

The Zealot will not listen to reasoned argument, is totally
inflexible, and is at the whim of emotions which leads them to
behave in otherwise irrational ways. Under normal
circumstances a person would not whip themselves for days on
end to prove that they believed in something, as the Zealot
does.

Buddha was quite clear about this approach to spiritual
belief, he said it was not positive. He actively encouraged
everyone to question what he said, and stated that one would
'know' whether the path was right or not. To blindly accept
what one was told, to follow doctrine, or to be more concerned
with the ritual than the spirit, was not the right approach.
Therefore strong emotional attachment to any particular belief
is also a negative thing.

Emotional weightings

How does emotion add weight to the framework and what is
it? Let us return to Barney. Barney has emotions, he shows
every sign of knowing:

◆ affection
◆ loyalty
◆ fear
◆ courage
◆ a whole range of 'feelings'.

What are feelings designed to do? If we go right back to the
beginning, they are simply instructions designed to protect the
organism. Over millions of years more and more complicated
frameworks developed, the essence of which could no longer
be analysed. Psychologists struggle to understand the reasons
we behave the way we do, and no wonder. They are trying to

disentangle a limitless web of frameworks, each with their connections to emotional values.

The major difference between Barney and us is that Barney never learnt to talk, and whereas he has some basic emotional responses similar to our own, he doesn't have the sophisticated emotions created by our ability to relate to ourselves, to the perceived 'I'. As soon as we knew we could be identified, and were able to relate to ourselves (which was what language gave us), we began to develop and enhance our basic emotional frameworks. This is the metaphysical interpretation of the fall from the Garden of Eden. The aim is to return through free will and understanding.

Breaking free of illusion

The more enmeshed we become with the self:

◆ the more tied we are
◆ the harder we cling
◆ the more we lose sight of the ultimate truth.

There may be a natural reluctance for most people to accept that emotion can be a bad thing. Get rid of emotion and we rid ourselves of our humanity. Look at Mr Spock in *Star Trek* – would we really like to be like him? It would be life Jim, but not as we know it. Zen has no room for the self, or not in the way we currently accept it. And the reason is, the self necessarily imposes preconditions on reality. The moment you begin to think about anything, you have already distorted whatever you were considering.

Where do we go from here?

Even by thinking about Zen you are distorting the issue, so what's the point? The point is that whenever you consider something new, you open up an area of the mind that is fresh and unhindered. The minute you 'think' about it, you are distorting it and imposing a burden on it.

> Zen is living at the centre where the thought occurs, before you have even given shape to it.

Supposing we could get back, behind the frameworks? Imagine them combining to make a wire frame ball, and at the very centre, at the core, there was a space. Into this space we drop a thought, and it is positively charged. It is pure, untouched, undistorted.

Now imagine the thought having to weave its way out through the frame, and as it does so, from the frame, it picks up negative ions. Its route is predetermined by the frameworks and the way they interlink. By the time it gets to the surface of the ball it is no longer what it was, it is weighed down by the ions. However much you like to think you are considering the original thought impartially, you are not.

Thinking, words and freedom

Here we have to return for a moment to words and the part they play. A word has to represent something. The fact that in your mind it represents something means that you have constructed a framework. So when a thought occurs, you 'think it' using words, which restricts us and leads us in a particular direction, and we don't want this. How can we be free if we are at the mercy of predetermined symbols?

◆ Supposing you could shock the mind into trying to think without words?

◆ Supposing it was possible to know, and yet not forge that knowing into a solid state?

Impossible? Not according to Zen. This is *satori*, or intuitive looking into. The purpose of the koans seems to be exactly that: to shock the mind, to cause a moment where the mind desperately searches for an answer it cannot possibly find, and in so doing breaks free of the pre-programmed way of constructing frameworks and reverts to intuitive thought.

Thinking intuitively

At the centre, in that place where thought originates, before it has been named, labelled and fixed, is a limitless universe. Everything is possible because nothing has been weighed down by the restrictions of the known. A glorious expanse of being exists, as it has always existed, un-named. So you see why, if you can describe it, then it is not Zen. In describing it we have used words, and you have used words to imagine it, so how can it be Zen? It is the *experience* and not the recollection or examination of the experience which is Zen.

Living in a Zen manner is to return to the pure essence of what we all are without analysing, expecting, anticipating, judging. How can one live like that? After all, in order to function we need to:

◆ judge situations
◆ look ahead
◆ take decisions.

This of course is true, but suppose you could do such things intuitively? Supposing you could just 'know'? You may have glimpsed the fish shining in the pond. If so, don't think about it too much, for then it will not be Zen.

Summary

Having looked at the nature of illusion and some ways of avoiding this illusion, here are some points to think about:

◆ If we create a world for ourselves, it is the one we have to live in. How good is the one you have created?
◆ How much do you live in the past, and how much do you live in the future?
◆ How open are you to new ideas, new concepts, or are you rigidly stuck in your point of view?
◆ Do you believe everything the media tells you? Do you enjoy reading about others' misfortunes? How much do you rely upon other people's opinions?
◆ How important is it to you to fit in with the current ideas of successful living?
◆ Do you cling to possessions, people, ideas – if so what happens when they are gone or in the case of ideas no longer prove to be true?
◆ Do you ever take the time to appreciate what you have at a particular moment?
◆ How aware are you of the structures through which your thoughts pass before they reach the surface of your mind?
◆ Do you ever stop thinking and allow your mind to go clear?

CHAPTER 7

Learning to Trust

T rust is the fundamental skill we learn in our first year of life, according to Erikson. But we continue to learn, understand and master trust throughout our life. Rather than feel that our life is ruined because we did not have a fully trusting environment to grow up in, we can value our understanding of what life is like without trust. Then we can fully appreciate it. The basis for healing from any trauma is to accept this perspective and move on.

Defining trust

To recap, the ego prefers and creates a state of fear which it can use to dominate and control. Fear prevents us trusting, and without trust we drive away that which we most desire in our life. If we conquer the ego we live in a state of trust, love and peace.

◆ We know that all our needs are being met endlessly.
◆ We know the truth about human concepts of limitation and lack – they do not exist.
◆ If limitations do not exist, there is nothing to fear and so we are able to live in peace, freedom and love.
◆ If there is nothing for the ego to latch on to, to create an illusion of fear, it has no power.

That's why it is important to recognise your own emotional energies. Are they predominantly fear or trust? And that will answer your question of why things that happen in your life happen to you. *They reflect back to you your own beliefs.* As you conquer the influences of ego, your life will improve.

Trusting subjective experience

Ultimately the only influence to trust in your life is yourself and your own knowledge. That is why it is so important to get back to accepting a perspective of solipsism. If you are offered an apple that looks really good, but are told that it is sour, how can you know? There is no proof until you yourself taste the apple and discover if it is sour to you. And what is sour for one person is not for another.

Our subjectivity shows we can all experience the same event with a different outcome, the apple is sour for some tastes but not for others.

Trusting emotions

Your emotions are your messengers. They inform you of your deepest unconscious beliefs and whether the experiences you are having feel comfortable or not. If we suppress the emotions we are putting the messenger in prison without ever looking at what the message is. So we are missing the point. The emotions are there to get us to respond, and then we can dismiss the emotion and make a choice of how to respond.

Trusting the evidence

What evidence do we need for knowing the truth about the apple and where does that come from? The problem is that to take the first bite, to find the truth, we have to take a chance, to trust the apple will not taste bad. We are usually too afraid that it might be a poisoned apple even though there is nothing to suggest it is, and all who have tasted similar apples are glad that they did. Once you have open-mindedly tasted the apple, you know the truth for yourself. Even if you subsequently pretend differently to yourself, it is only a denial of a truth that you cannot face. The trouble is that sometimes tasting that metaphorical apple challenges everything your human life is built on. This makes the ego feel very threatened and we react with fear.

Case Study _____

Robin had trained in conventional medicine, and practised successfully for his whole life. He had achieved considerable status for contributions to his chosen area of specialism. His health deteriorated in later life and an ulcer appeared on his leg. Nothing seemed to heal this ulcer. A chance meeting leads to an offer of energy or spiritual healing. He accepts it on impulse, without having time to think, and experiences some relief. But then he realises the implications of that healing. It challenges his whole basis of understanding life up to this point, the premise upon which his own success is built. Suddenly that healing becomes much more threatening and he refuses further treatment. He prefers to continue in pain than accept something which takes him into uncharted territory. A week later the dressing is again changed and eventually the leg does heal. This becomes the explained source of the healing even though changes of dressing had done nothing beforehand. _____

Getting over the intellectual barrier is hard and very frightening for some people. In their fear they will seek every means to demonstrate they are right. But why put so much energy into denying something they believe is not real? Why bother?

The strength of denial is a recognition that the experience is real and a measure of the fear of those implications. In this way have many cruelties been created and truths been denied, but ultimately truth will always survive the onslaught of denial.

> As Plato said, ultimately there is never enough evidence for those who do not wish to believe and there is no evidence needed for those who do.

So if someone denies the validity of your experiences and says 'I don't believe it, prove it to me', their ego is talking. Don't be hurt or upset if this happens, it is not you they are rejecting it is their fear of what you represent.

Hidden agendas

For most people the hidden agenda is the fear of accepting a truth that challenges their concept of 'how life is'. They believe they will lose something valuable rather than gain something far more precious than they can imagine. Think of the monkey trap. The ego is the origin. So if you deny personal experience as proof, it is an ego position.

Surely some things do need proving? If you come back to the principle that thought creates reality, nothing is impossible, so why should anything need proof? We can accept it, even if it

is outside our own experiences. An open mind is the
alternative.

Labelling experiences

Using terms such as 'good' and 'bad' experience is subjective,
as is positive or negative. If we learn about trusting
appropriately, we need to learn that trust must be placed wisely
and with consideration, but also with openness and generosity.
We are all doing the best we can with what we know in any given
situation.

To criticise someone for letting us down and showing us
when not to trust is unkind. That person has been just as
valuable a teacher in our life as someone who shows when to
trust. All they did was to demonstrate their level of mastery, as
an example of what to do and what not to do. So negative
experiences are not negative at all. They are simply more
challenging and uncomfortable, because they confront us with
our mistakes, so we label them negative.

Labelling our self

Difficult experiences are the cause of all our problems because
we allow them to be. We tend to feel that we are a 'victim of
someone else's bad behaviour'. What we are doing is ignoring
our own lack of competence at that skill, or we would not be a
victim of anything. We would have known enough to avoid
experiencing their inappropriate behaviour.

> If someone treats us inappropriately once, that is their
> responsibility. But if we say nothing and they repeat it, it is
> ours.

Our ignorance is not a defence. It is the evidence we need to
complete our own training in these skills. We consider
ourselves the victim of circumstance and that thought becomes
our reality. The victim attitude is common to everyone at some
level. Can you honestly say you have never considered yourself
the victim of circumstance. You will probably recognise this
feeling.

Try it now   Consider these three phrases:

- *Poor* me.
- It isn't my *fault*.
- I couldn't *help* it.

Now look at the italicised words. What does *poor* mean? It means lack, being without – money, good health, friends, whatever. It means not having. This is the opposite of abundance. *Fault* means right or wrong. *Help* means not taking responsibility. So we have a choice:

- develop a 'poor' mentality where we 'need help' and see 'fault'
- develop an abundance mentality where we see learning, growth, opportunity and responsibility.

After this exercise, make a conscious decision to start to recognise your lack mentality and change it.

Why we find trust so hard

One of the fundamental cornerstones of trust is honesty. This includes:

- our personal honesty with ourselves
- what we are hiding from
- the honesty of society around us.

Buddhism embodies this principle within two of its eight noble pathways, **right thought** and **right speech**. Our society has lost sight of what truth really is. Socially acceptable behaviour includes several forms of dishonesty.

Self becomes hidden in a shell of untruth around us (see Figure 9), and we collude with it.

- Without honesty we cannot trust.
- Without trust we live in fear.
- Living in fear keeps us separate from our true self and allows the ego power over us.

Is it any wonder we find it so hard to trust anything that we

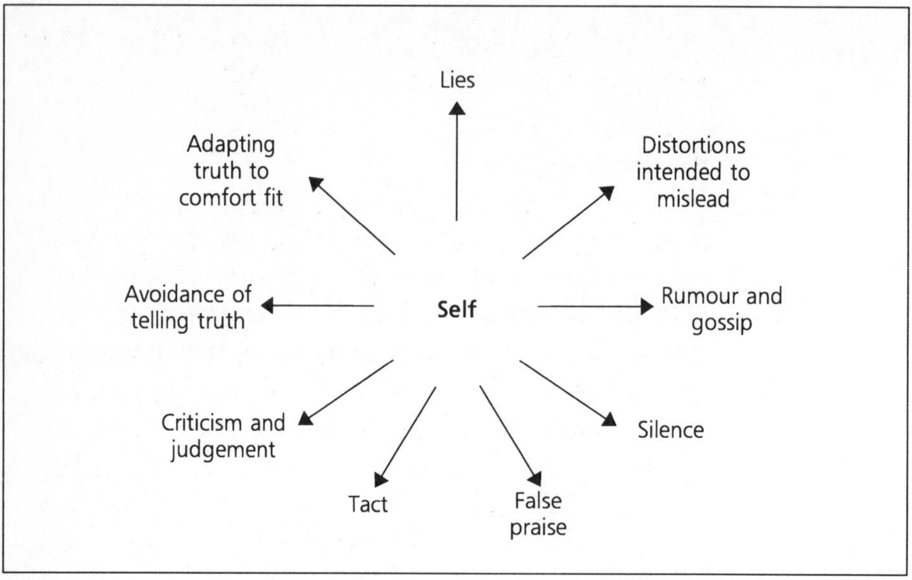

Fig. 9. Right thought, right speech, honesty.

do not feel we have some control over? To speak our own truth is considered antisocial and unkind. So we are stuck in a belief that honesty is inappropriate and yet we need to find some way of trusting. There are many reasons why speaking with open honesty is considered rude.

We are all doing our best

One reason we fear truth is because we fear criticism and judgement. The simplicity of this sub-title removes the need to judge, to fear criticism or to feel any shame or guilt. It is the basis for trust and counters the victim attitude completely. It embodies no attachments, no pre-judgements and no criticisms for self-archetypes or for others. It is all a degree of skill – no right or wrong – all allowed to be different and conform to our own paradigms or models of reality.

> All judgements are denying the right to make mistakes and to learn from them.

Our judgement is always based on a subjective understanding. What we can never do is know the full story behind that person, because even that person has changed from the person they were five minutes ago.

Trusting the process of change

Buddhism teaches the concept of continuous and absolute change. The person you are today is not the same person you were yesterday. There are aspects that remain, there's a continuity in consciousness, but it is not completely the same person. Even in the last ten minutes you have read things that may have changed you from before you opened this book – slightly. You are not the same person, you have changed, just by listening to the ideas we have been discussing. So we can accept this process of continuous and perpetual change, that nothing is permanent including ourselves. Then there is no judgement.

Trusting the nature of impermanence

We are always growing and changing and we go through the seasons of our life. Each year we celebrate our birthdays and each year we change. Apart from becoming a year older chronologically, we grow and change in every way, through all our experiences.

There are many ways of seeing age:

◆ emotional
◆ intellectual
◆ chronological
◆ social
◆ physical.

Age itself is a human construct, it is simply part of the much bigger process of change. Some people may be emotionally more mature and yet maintain a youthful body. So what is their age? We all differ.

Change creates and fills its own spaces

The laws of nature say that if you create a vacuum, matter will rush in to fill that space and the same is true in our lives. If we fear losing something as a result of changes, or we fear being

less than we are, then we are actually filling a space that could
be filled with something positive. We can fill the space with
our own negative beliefs or we can release them and allow
something positive to come in. We must let go and make space
for:

◆ new feelings
◆ new thoughts
◆ new ideas
◆ changes
◆ new attitudes and perceptions.

If we allow it to happen, and go with the flow, we no longer
need to feel ashamed of who we were and what we have done
because that person no longer exists. Right here, right now
maybe we wouldn't make the same mistakes. We can all think
of many things we have done that we would never do now. But
at the time it was all we knew for getting ourself in or out of
situations where we felt trapped, unhappy, or insecure and
didn't have the understanding we have now.

To judge our self on something that we did then is
incredibly unkind. We have no reason to feel guilty or ashamed
of who we were, or to feel possessive of anything we have for
fear of losing it. If we lose it something better will come in,
just as we have become a better person by letting go of the
past. We have moved on. Once we have learned to trust the
process of change, it becomes much easier.

Compassionately forgiving ourselves

What we must always remember, when struggling with these
emotions, is to be compassionate with ourselves. It does take
time to recognise these feelings. The aim is always to keep
working with our consciousness. It is important to be
compassionate both with ourselves and with other people
experiencing these things around us.

The choice is how we respond from now on, and trusting
that whatever we choose we will learn from. This is a very
strong Buddhist and metaphysical teaching, that *it is our choice*
how we deal with these things. We can choose:

◆ to be harsh on ourselves

- ◆ to be compassionate
- ◆ to carry on as we have always done
- ◆ to make changes.

Once we recognise that our fears are illusions we can start laughing at ourselves. Gently, compassionately, good-humouredly, saying 'why on earth am I doing this to myself, beating myself up with shame, guilt, anger and fear. Who is having fun, because it ain't me, so why am I doing it?' Just make those choices to let it go. We can move into a state of trusting that, whatever happens, we will achieve whatever our higher self wants us to. That achievement will teach us the true meaning of fulfilment and love.

Taking the plunge

There is no point in deciding that you will trust everything immediately and start right away. Trust is a skill and needs to be understood on all levels. People and situations will not always conform to our expectations and we might feel that we cannot trust them. Yet you trust that the force of gravity will keep your feet firmly on the planet surface. If you lose balance and fall, you feel shaken. Your trust in your physical stability is momentarily upset. So what can and do we trust and what not?

Try it now   Think back to the apple and taking a bite. Start by thinking of all the things you take for granted each day, eg:

- ◆ When you flick a light switch, you trust it will connect the supply of electricity and create light for you. You usually notice it only if it does not work.
- ◆ You trust in your ability to co-ordinate eyes and hands, legs etc.

Make a list of all the things you do trust each day and think about what they have in common. What is your trust based on?

You usually find that your trust is based on what you know you can cope with, or do, things that are reliable. Reliable things include:

- ◆ Other people in a general sense. It is more than likely that they will let you down because they are human and that is what humans do. It is their best but not what we would like.

♦ Your own resilience. Experiences have shown you how much you can or cannot cope with. As you take increasing responsibility for your own life, you can trust yourself more and more.

♦ Life does not always work out as we want it to, but it usually works out OK.

♦ Change occurs whether we expect it or not, whether we would choose it or not, whether we like it or not.

If we can begin to recognise these aspects of experience as things we can trust, and to see them as desirable or positive, then we find that trust is not an issue. We recognise that
♦ our own experiences
♦ our own opinions and responses
♦ our own approach to life,
are all that count.

Once we stop looking outside ourselves for something to make us feel safe and start to recognise the power we have within us, to manage all that life offers, we find there is nothing but trust to experience. In Buddhist terms it is called **being your own refuge**. Mastery of this skill in life means:

♦ Your sense of self is not subject to behaviours and feelings of other people.

♦ Your sense of balance in life is continuous and unshakeable.

♦ Your sense of fulfilment is internal and cannot be threatened by anything outside yourself.

♦ You have no need to criticise others or to judge, because you know nothing is 'wrong'.

♦ Your life does not carry burdens of guilt and shame, of fear and anger because you are at peace with yourself.

♦ Your energy is all available to you to manifest whatever you want in life without ego conflict.

♦ Your sense of purpose and direction is unshaken by the unexpected.

So if you want to find your goals in life, start trusting as much as you can and work to increase it each day. Do not allow yourself to be fooled by evidence that suggests you should not trust and remember to invest your trust in things that are principles. These are the only form of permanence we can rely on. Using falsely placed trust as a reason not to trust further is self-defeating and pointless. It is also very common.

Summary

Trust is a unique aspect of love. It is one of the foundation stones in understanding the full meaning of love. It is the fundamental lesson we learn in our first year of life and continue to learn throughout our lives. It is an excellent example of how mirroring works, that our experience will mirror back to us our level of and understanding of trust.

- ◆ Trust enables you to flow through life without fear.
- ◆ Underneath all the other principles, the one thing you can rely on, and trust completely, is the nature of change and impermanence.
- ◆ Learning to trust means letting go of negative beliefs such as criticism and judgement, right and wrong.
- ◆ Trust means accepting life is as it is, and everyone is in it together – we are all part of the whole and there is no competition.

| A pattern creates order and organisation from seemingly random events. | # Recognising Repeating Patterns |

What are patterns?

L ife is a journey, a gradual development of the individual through experience, the various stages and events of life. From the very young child learning to walk, talk and communicate, to the last breath, we never stop learning. The key to a more fulfilled life is based on a recognition of this need to continue learning and being open to experiences in all areas of our lives and our selves. The purpose of life is to be happy and we need to learn what that means. So we learn what makes us unhappy and what true happiness really is, and what is false or illusory happiness. Repeating life patterns are the lessons we use to learn this. We can never avoid the lessons even if we ignore the learning. We just get put back a grade each time.

Always learning new skills

When a child of 1 first pulls themselves up to stand and walk alone, they will fall many times before they are able to walk, run, jump and hop with confidence. As adults we are still learning. We still need to make mistakes in order to learn properly. Not only are mistakes unavoidable, they are essential to the experience of learning.

> You cannot appreciate the value of balanced, confident movement unless you know what it feels like to fall. You cannot know the importance of any aspect of your life unless you understand the meaning of its absence.

Why repeating patterns?

The human brain is designed to form patterns to make routine and regular activities more efficient. It is an adaptive quality that serves us well in many aspects of life. Imagine if you had to learn how to get dressed each morning, as if you had never done it before. What effect would it have on your life if you had to do everything from scratch each time? So patterns allow us to learn and retain skills and ideas. However, the problem sets in when we hold onto ideas and routines that are not in our best interests, but because they are familiar we think they are 'right'. They make us feel safe, but that is an illusion and we are just stuck in a repeating pattern. In reality the pattern only persists until we have learned a better way of behaving.

How do you know if you are stuck in a pattern? The truth is that we are all stuck somewhere in our life. The skill is in recognising and taking opportunities to change.

◆ Do you seem to be going round in circles?
◆ Do some parts of your life seem endlessly repetitive?
◆ Do you feel that you are stepping out of the frying pan into the fire all the time?
◆ Do you sometimes feel that life is conspiring against you?

As we highlighted before, if you keep doing what you've always done you'll keep getting what you've always got.

What is happening?

The main thing about life is that it teaches us endlessly *how to be happy*. Whatever we need to examine and address within is a mirror image of what is occurring to us all round. Whatever we dislike in our life, that is the evidence we need to start the process of change.

One common area for repetitions of life patterns is in relationships. Several explanations for this are offered by various schools of psychology, but one that makes the most sense is that people often find a partner who reflects their parents' qualities in some way.

Attracting similar energies

Whatever emotions we have inside us create an energy field around us, commonly called our **aura**. These energies are created by the small electrical impulses running through our nervous system. This contains our conscious and unconscious feelings as an energy field around our body. These are not just the emotions we feel on the surface, but all the feelings suppressed inside our bodies from old hurts not yet released and healed. Each energy vibration attracts appropriate energies to them. So if you hold a lot of angry energy inside you, you will attract angry energy into your life as direct expression of anger.

Although the experience of this attraction may be very uncomfortable and distressing to go through, it has one very positive result. That is, to enable us to recognise and address our own inner emotions. Once we release our own anger there will be little or no anger coming towards us in life. And so on. So if you have problems with poverty, stop affirming how poor you are, stop seeing the glass half empty. The best case study for this principle comes from the New Testament and the poor widow with her last drop of oil. It was all that she had left but she gave it anyway, and when she poured the oil did not stop flowing. This is declared a miracle but it is the principle of abundance in evidence.

◆ If you affirm poverty, and justify this by saying 'look how little I have got', you will perpetuate that reality. You are stuck in a repeating pattern of lack.

◆ If you affirm how much you do have, whatever it is, you increase your abundance accordingly.

Like the song 'I ain't Got No, I got Life' if that is all you have, celebrate that and see what comes to you. Do not celebrate in order to receive, celebrate from true gratitude. Life will give you the opportunity if you allow it. The universe wants you to be happy. The rest is up to you.

What does this mean in reality?

◆ If you find yourself always caught in situations of aggression or anger – you are being advised to resolve your own inner anger.

◆ If you find that people in your life do not value you enough and seem only interested in what you can do for them not what they can do for you – you are being advised to start to care for yourself first.

◆ If you find that every idea that you have which seems very good initially seems to crumble away and come to nothing – you are being advised to believe in your ideas and your ability to carry them through.

◆ If you feel that no one understands you and fails to give you what you want in life – you are being advised to start to understand yourself and take responsibility for meeting your own needs.

The universe wants us to learn

The other aspect of this is that each time we go round in the same patterns it seems to get bigger and more distressing. This happens for a reason. The more we fail to recognise our patterns, the more we accumulate the energy associated with that pattern inside us. The positive aspect of this is that eventually we will notice what is happening and do something to change. Any change will create a new energy. But the more we are aware of which energies we attract into our life, the more we are able to transform our life by transforming our own emotional energy.

How can it change?

The simple act of recognising that we are caught in repeating patterns is the first step.

> There are no mistakes in life, there are only lessons to be learned. When one lesson has stopped, many more will take its place. Each leads us closer to happiness.

Each lesson has to be learned in many ways throughout the length of the spirit's journey at this level. We refer to the individual life as a spirit journey because it represents the inner self, the core of our being, of conscious awareness, rather than our physical identity. All healing philosophies have this basic principle of learning at their centre.

Other people are your teachers

Another important truth to remember, while exploring your

patterns, is that others are merely mirrors of you. Every response you have to another person is based on how you feel inside about yourself.

If you do not have a strong feeling about something in relationship to yourself, you will not mind that attribute in other people. This is often the basis of transferring our problems with ourselves onto other people and avoiding the exploration of ourselves, Freud's ego defence of **transference**. We cannot blame other people for our own experiences and yet we do so all the time. In fact this is probably going to make you disagree with me because you have so much evidence and support from others to justify the contrary. But others are a mirror of ourselves and we attract people who will teach us. We are stuck until we learn our patterns of attraction and move on to the next stage of understanding ourselves.

> You cannot like or dislike anything in others that you do not like or dislike in yourself.

Starting with honesty as an example, in order to understand each lesson, we need to experience what it is like to live:
- ◆ with honesty from others
- ◆ without honesty from others
- ◆ with honesty for others
- ◆ without honesty for others
- ◆ with honesty for self
- ◆ without honesty for self.

The same applies to the whole list below and any others you can think of. These lessons can be learned in lots of small steps or in one or two very big ones. This is one of the rational explanations for the existence of pain and suffering. This dimensional approach to learning allows us to recognise each of the lessons, and there may be many more than we have listed.

Try it now   Using the above list consider your own life and each of these areas of learning with as much honesty as possible. Decide which areas you have covered and which you are still covering. Take each lesson area and examine it from each of the six aspects by thinking of an example and what it has taught you.

This is not dwelling in the past but using it constructively to learn from. Make a note of the areas where you have reached success in all aspects and the areas in which you still experience difficulties.

◆ love
◆ patience
◆ trust
◆ compassion
◆ honesty
◆ respect
◆ generosity
◆ creativity
◆ health
◆ responsibility
◆ forgiveness
◆ knowledge
◆ intuition
◆ empathy
◆ communication
◆ prosperity.

One of the best ways to know that you have covered any learning is to recognise you have no problems in this area and you know exactly where you stand. For instance, if you have absolute harmony with truth, and all six aspects of it, then you probably have nothing more to learn in this area of your life.

Patterns exist in themes but also in areas of our life. A key to recognising where you are presently stuck is to look at the areas of your life and see what is happening in them all. The following list is fairly comprehensive but add your own if you wish.

◆ work and educational achievement
◆ self-expression through creativity
◆ relationships with partners
◆ relationships with close friends
◆ relationships with parents
◆ material possessions and comfort
◆ relationships with children and other close family members
◆ making new relationships with any of the above
◆ illness and well-being – emotional and physical
◆ any others you can think of.

Consider which areas are successful and require little effort from you and which ones require a lot of effort.

Expecting the worst

Why do things happen to good people as well as bad people? The answer is that it is nothing to do with good or bad, that is a judgemental opinion and is subjective. It is based on opinions and social beliefs that change. We have to accept there is no good and bad as such, just experiences that teach us more about abundance and happiness.

If you expect problems, you give them energy and they occur because of that energy. You made them come true. Some people seem to drift through life with never a gloomy thought and life just seems to give them an easy ride. If you think positively then even the problems are less and are more of a challenge than a disaster. If you think negatively in areas of your life, you will experience the results of those thoughts. We get into patterns of thinking which re-create themselves endlessly, eg victim attitudes (Chapter 6).

Using your brain

Patterns tend to occur mainly in the left brain, the domain of the ego. Creative and intuitive thought originates from the right brain which can 'see' patterns and the whole picture. Intuitive thinking is our best tool for recognising what we need to change and how. The mind is loosely divided into two halves of the brain:

Left brain
- linear thought
- logical processes
- information analysis
- details
- grammar
- language
- recognition of parts
- sequences of actions.

Right brain
- whole picture – overview
- pictures or emotions
- rhythm
- patterns of words, prose, poetry or song
- creativity
- innovation and imagination
- language recognition
- visualisation and dreaming
- intuitive thought.

Sometimes the two halves of the brain are working together and sometimes they are not.

(a) If your thoughts and intentions say one thing, and your actions another, it is because of this lack of co-operation between the two brains, or the conscious and sub-conscious minds.

(b) If your conscious ideals and subconscious desires work against each other, pushing you in opposite directions, this results in a lot of effort with very little accomplishment.

So your goals and desires may not be congruent with your words and actions. However, as your conscious ideals and subconscious desires unite to work together, pushing and building in the same direction, there is no limit to what you can achieve. The important thing is to recognise the areas of your life where there is contradiction and what the directional pulls are (refer back to the work you did in Chapters 1 and 2).

Breaking patterns

In order to break a repeating pattern we must change what we are doing. Changes have a domino effect and we often fear to change one thing because we unconsciously recognise that it will have this effect. We therefore prefer to continue with what we know.

Some people go to great lengths to convince themselves of their desire to change. They spend years in therapy yet nothing changes, but they can say 'look how much commitment I have made to therapy, I am trying'. The truth is that they are doing everything they can to convince themselves that they are trying to make changes but they will achieve very little because of their resistance. Trying means failing, it carries within it the concept of failure. So either do it or don't do it.

Coping with change

We are all subject to changes but mostly we resist changes we have not consciously chosen. The familiar is the most comfortable. Change is inevitable; teaching from Buddhism and metaphysics show that change is the basis of life. Remember the apple:

◆ it does not exist as an apple forever, neither does it stop existing

◆ it changes daily, through ripening and decay

◆ consider when the apple began to exist, before it was a flower, then a bud and before that a twig on a tree

◆ the sun and rain and soil have all had a part in the making of this apple, as have insects in pollinating it.

When did the apple begin, from the point of pollination or before? Was not the potential for that apple already within the seed from which the tree grew and will it not carry that potential into the ground or digestive tract of its consumer? But the seed had to stop being a seed in order to become a new tree, to create new apples. Will the seed in the centre of the apple not create another tree from which more apples will grow? We will come back to this example later on as it is a useful metaphor for our life. But for now consider that we are as an apple: we do not remain the same, each day we ripen and mature in the sun and the rain.

Try it now   Think about the changes that occurred in your life over the last two years. Even make some notes. Consider how they have affected you. Don't put a judgement on those changes, no good or bad, just note them and their effects on your life. Follow those changes right through to now. Put down all the experiences just as they are. Different experiences give us different perspectives, so just allow your self to follow them through, making as many connections as possible. You may find that some of these experiences are still causing you to feel rather than to just know but do your best to simply observe. You will notice that changes *have* occurred – in some cases huge ones. If you repeat this exercise with a five-year period it will be even more obvious how change has benefited your experience. Now that you have your list, consider what has each change actually brought you.

The impersonal nature of experience

Remember that it is not the change that brings us any difficulty, it is our **resistance** to change which causes our pain. Any experience is neutral, ie it is non-personal. It is our subjective interpretation of change that creates our emotional difficulties. This is a principle. Thus two people may receive the same experience and yet both perceive it as quite different, one feeling it was a wonderful opportunity and the other feeling a victim of fate.

Resistance is useless

All change is for our good because all change brings some learning and growth. If we resist change, we resist the natural flow of our whole life and will consequently feel that life is against us. But the reality is that *we* are against life, we are against the natural flow and development of our lives.

We may want some changes, they are the easy ones to cope with. It is the changes we fear that cause us pain by resisting them.

◆ If we accept change as an essential and irrevocable part of life, we are able to lessen the pain to ourselves and find the gift in each change.

◆ If we can see the potential in the change we experience a small amount of conflict and accept this as part of the process.

It is like moving house or changing job. If we have chosen to make the change we accept that there will be some difficulty, but we also trust our ability to cope with it and not feel threatened by its effects on us. We can go with the flow much more comfortably. If it is imposed we feel conflict, victimised.

Seeing love in all experience

By opening our perception, we can recognise we have gained:

◆ understanding that we could not have got in any other way

◆ understanding of human experience

◆ a greater understanding of ourselves and what we are capable of

◆ how well we can hurt ourselves

◆ how well we allow other people to hurt us.

That is still a great gift because if we choose to accept the lesson, we never have to repeat it. To fully understand a facet of experience we *need to experience it in both positive and negative ways* – or rather, challenging and joyful ways, since they are both positive in that they both teach equally. Indeed it could be argued that the master teacher is the most painful experience, so perhaps we should welcome them the most.

> In order to learn anything, you have to experience it.

Once you have experienced all six dimensions – three withs and three withouts, you will really begin to understand what, for instance, trust or respect means. But until you recognise the learning you are being offered you will continue to experience those difficulties in your life. It is really up to you to accept changes and see what they are teaching you.

More than one dimension at a time

Once we have learned to live without trust in our lives then we have to learn to live *with* it and sometimes this can be as hard. So usually we are being shown all six dimensions at the same time but in different aspects of our lives. If someone somewhere is betraying our trust you can be sure that somewhere else there is an equally good teacher of the opposite and so on. If we recognise these connections, and understand what we are contributing to our own situation, we can begin to change that within us. By changing that within us we create positive change in our life.

Change is ultimately good because it is intending to lead us to a life of abundance, based on a sound understanding of what that really is.

◆ First we have to understand what it is within us that attracts to us the lack experiences – the situation where trust is being betrayed – and then to fully awaken to the importance of trust in all its aspects.

◆ As we become more able to trust ourself and others we find life is filled with trustworthy people, but if a few non-trustworthy people come along we can spot them and are unaffected by their games and strategies.

♦ We all have to learn each of these lessons, so we should never criticise or judge those who have yet to learn what we already know. That is hypocrisy; others had to cope with the behaviour which resulted from our own previous ignorance.

Once you see how much the changes in your life have led you on, then you can begin to welcome all changes and recognise that nothing was imposed on you, you attracted them. You needed to learn that lesson as a stage of development of your own consciousness.

Making choices to change

One of the biggest lessons we have to learn is to trust our own intuition. This allows us to make better choices in life and choose the most effective way of living and changing. Our intuition will show us what we need to learn from each situation if we are prepared to listen to it. Listening is an essential skill. We need to learn:

♦ to listen
♦ what it feels like not to be listened to
♦ to listen to our own intuition
♦ how much potential wisdom we miss by not listening to others.

Change as avoidance of a lesson

Recognising the need for change, and even developing the desire for change, is not the same as being addicted to it. Some people make drastic changes in their lives very often and never give themselves a chance to see something through to the end. Change can give the illusion of progress, but change for its own sake rarely brings anything into our life except instability and upheaval.

Some people need to feel a sense of crisis in order to feel alive. They are addicted to the adrenaline. This kind of change is very powerful and dramatic, and can seem to be dynamic.

But change has to be followed by a period of consolidation, however short that is, so that the benefits of the change are in place before we move on. Change for its own sake rarely teaches us anything other than how to cope with change. Not a worthless lesson but missing the point.

When we realise we are doing this, we can stop creating change for its own sake. If this sounds like you then take the learning and move on, before you change your life away into nothing of any substance.

Change will always be constructive if we make the best use of it. It is part of this thing called choice and free will. It is our choice whether or not we learn from our experience.

Resistance hurts more

Change is inevitable. Resistance is like a piece of tightly stretched elastic.

◆ The harder we pull the more it hurts when it finally snaps back on us.
◆ We can keep the elastic gently taught but not stretched so that it can move, but never snaps back on us.
◆ We can make our progress through life as smooth or as filled with turmoil as we choose.

This does not mean that we avoid life, which is many people's way of avoiding turmoil. They keep their heads down and don't put a foot wrong, take risks or confront the system, they live a half-life and never really discover their full potential or abundance. They live in fear of change and seek to avoid it by creating illusions of security. What security is there in a relationship where both parties remain from fear and duty rather than from complete freedom of choice and because they want to be there and nowhere else? Fear of change creates this illusion of security, even though everyone also knows it is a flimsy reality at best and very easily destroyed.

Real security

Security never depends on money or other people. It depends on our ability to cope with change and whatever life is likely to throw at us, and more than that – to enjoy it, to take it in both hands and savour its freshness and poignancy.

> We can step back to watch changes taking place, observe them as if they are the river passing us by whilst we watch, rather than become caught up in their icy torrent.

This is based on a Buddhist technique aimed at non-attachment which we cover in depth in Chapter 11.

Most fear of change is based on thoughts of past and future, rarely of the immediate present. If we are fully aware of the present we cannot feel fear, we are either dealing with something or not. If we are fully occupied with the now we are unavailable to unnecessary worry about the future or thoughts of the past.

So fear of change and resistance to it is based on a preoccupation with the past which is over, and the future which is yet to come, and may not be as our thoughts suggest.

Try it now You may want to record this for yourself.

Close your eyes and take a couple of breaths...and with each breath out allow yourself to drift a little deeper into a state of deep relaxation...focusing on your thoughts and feelings... allow them to be like the river...flowing past your mind... just allow them to be and watch them...every so often you may seem to find an interesting thought...an enlightening thought flowing with the rest...notice it and reflect on it... then let it also pass by...you might find thoughts of rejection of these teachings...that you find it too much for now, you are not ready to hear this yet...or resistant to hearing this and what it means in your life...resistant to letting go of beliefs which keep you trapped in the rapids...whatever you find just let it pass...all of it...tell yourself firmly to let them all go for now...you can come back to any of it when you want to, if you think there is value to be gained in this but for now just let it all pass you by. Begin to see it all as a dancing stream over the rocks, bubbling in the sunshine, sparkling clear and beautiful...full of life...full of enthusiasm for life... supporting life...sit and enjoy this stream passing you by... knowing that you have chosen this in your life...chosen to live this stream, to live with its course and currents...And equally you have a choice to change...So now consider what you life is showing you...What you might lose and what you could gain if you learn to let go and allow change to come into your life...See yourself in a few weeks with these changes firmly in place...and see all the positive things which this change has brought into your life...Make a commitment now to yourself, to ask your higher self to guide you through the changes...to show you the learning and to let things go...so that your life moves effortlessly on into whatever comes next... and allow yourself to feel the full fun of the adventure.

Now open your eyes.

Watching the process

Sometimes it is quite possible to recognise the changes going on inside us, to really feel them and be aware of them. These moments of such joyful lucidity are rare to begin with. But as you continue working with it all you can find:

♦ you are monitoring your own progress and seeing what you need to do next

♦ you see the issue you are being shown in life

♦ it doesn't always lessen the discomfort completely

♦ it does help you to see and welcome it

♦ it does help you to drop the victim attitude and take life with a positive attitude

♦ sometimes you can even see yourself resisting and recognising the gift at the same time, which is an extraordinary feeling.

The important thing is not to lose our sense of humour when it comes to our own lives. We would probably laugh at our experiences if they were in a sitcom but in real life, it's quite different. Learning to laugh our way through changes and treat life rather as an enjoyable fairground ride is the best way to deal with it all. Sometimes life offers us this chance to see things with utter clarity but we must still remember that what we have experienced is a sudden leap in consciousness, not all there is to know. Wherever we have reached there will always be deeper levels to explore. But this is the best part of the whole adventure, knowing that there is always more, and if we learn the lessons openly and without resistance, the changes lead us on to better things.

Changes mean letting go and making room for the new

We fear change because we are afraid it may cause us to lose something that we believe we need. That thing may even be self-abusive, like a violent relationship. We fear that if we give something up we will be left empty. This is never the case. We will always fill the space left by letting something go in our life but again it is up to us to create that filler. We can follow a pattern: fill it with our bitterness, fear and anger so that we do not allow anything good into our life and believe our self to be the victim.

Summary

All people have patterns in their lives. The patterns are not the problem, they are a natural way of learning about life. It is only when we keep repeating them that the problem occurs for us.

- ◆ Patterns are created by the refusal to learn lessons in life.
- ◆ Patterns repeat until you learn their message and make changes in your life.
- ◆ When one lesson ends another has already begun, the basis for perpetual change.
- ◆ Change does not cause problems, it is resistance to change which causes discomfort and pain.
- ◆ Fear of change causes you to miss out on much of what life has to offer and creates an illusion of security and continuity.

Lessons are gifts from the universe because they are opportunities to change.

Learning the Lessons – Recognising Control

We are here to live and part of the process of living is to learn how to do it better, to become more skilful at managing our experiences and ourselves. In order to learn anything, a context is needed. Everything that happens to us, in every aspect of our life, is exactly that – *an opportunity to learn.*

What we are learning is more about our true natures, who or what we really are. Once we begin consciously seeking answers to that question, life becomes very interesting. When we fail to recognise the lesson we are being shown, we repeat the lesson until we get it right. That is the basis of the previous chapter. So why is it so hard to learn?

The principal lesson we are here to understand is the true nature of love and what that means in all its dimensions. As an aspect of love, trust is equally important. So are happiness, health and abundance.

> Lessons are learned in relation to experiences and other people. That is the principal function for relationships and the basis for our desire to have relationships of all kinds.

The opposite of love is fear and that manifests in many forms. We have already looked at anger, guilt, shame and jealousy. The need to **control** is another very unskilful behaviour based on fear, especially showing a lack of trust and acceptance. Everyone experiences this in some way, it is just a question of degree. This is what makes it harder for us to learn the lessons that experience shows us.

What is control?

Control is based on the idea that life, and people, cannot be trusted to get things right on their own. Whose idea of right though? The opposite of trust is mistrust, a fear-based emotion, so control is based in fear and manifests in feelings, thoughts, and attitudes. It usually comes from:

◆ fear of change
◆ fear of loss
◆ fear of rejection
◆ fear of being wrong and being rejected for it
◆ fear of being right and being rejected for it.

Most of us feel a need to know where we stand with our friends, with our partners or lovers, husbands, wives, children, perhaps with other members of our family, bosses, colleagues etc because:

◆ If we know where we stand, we feel confident.
◆ We want to make sure we have a good handle on everything – we want a sense of knowing where everything is and how it/you will behave.
◆ We prefer a sense of knowing how to control it all.
◆ We want to feel able to assess what is going to happen next.

Like all things in this lovely universe, it doesn't always work like that. The sun is always shining but sometimes there's a cloud or two in the way, or it's shining on the other half of the planet. You *never* know what is going to happen next. Sometimes we feel as if we do, and sometimes we don't, and that is the tricky bit. That is the fun bit if you like, the roller coaster ride.

There are two types of control behaviours:

◆ **active** – when we actively try to make things/people go as we plan them
◆ **passive** – when we allow other people to take control of our life and blame them when it goes wrong.

When things don't work out as we want them to we get angry, sometimes to the point of violence, or we become possessive or jealous, full of anxiety or phobias, or depressed. This is the basis of all emotional games.

Extreme forms of control

Phobia is an extreme desire to control a situation and a total experience of fear focused on one aspect of life you can't control. For example:

♦ Spiders represent our complete lack of control because they move with speed and silence. We cannot predict them.

♦ Agoraphobia, not being able to go out, is a fear of not being able to control, and therefore cope with, what is 'out there'.

Often phobias result from a shock, or a challenging or frightening experience that we have not released and forgiven. Whatever the cause, they highlight our predisposition towards fear. Fear of not being in control leads to games and manipulations, to meet these safety needs through other people and make us feel safe. A good example of the control factor in phobia is in the way people behave in relationships.

Case Study _____

Jane has been agoraphobic for years. Every time she starts to get better, making progress with her fears, she has a sudden relapse. When the whole family go for family therapy, it turns out that her husband Mark is insecure about his wife leaving him for someone else. He has kept her emotionally blocked by behaving in ways that made it better for her to stay inside. Then he could feel safe and be the martyr who has to do everything to care for this agoraphobic wife. So his low self-esteem was the problem, not her agoraphobia. Her agoraphobia was based in his need to control her because he feared she would leave him. He only felt safe if she was isolated. And she wanted him to be loving towards her, so she unconsciously complied with the game. Then Mark felt more powerful and secure by being the patient, martyr husband who coped with this agoraphobic wife. Looked at another way, Jane passively controlled Mark by being dependent, 'if you want me to stay in you will have to . . . '. Mark actively controlled Jane by behaving in unpleasant ways that made it seem 'not worth wanting independence'.

Being out of control

Sometimes the need to control manifests as an out-of-control pattern of behaviour as well.

♦ Most addictions occur when you have completely lost

control and believe that the focus of your addiction has power over you, more than you have yourself. This is passive control.

♦ Some extreme emotional behaviours, including violence, are a result of the individual being out of control emotionally. They actively control others through fear.

One of the ways to deal with the control or out of control feelings is to focus on being in the now. When you are fully in the present you cannot have negative feelings about what might happen.

> If you focus on the present, on the right here right now, you are too busy living with and dealing with what is happening, so there is nothing to control.

There are several basic reasons for feeling in or out of control:

♦ You can feel out of control because of powerful emotions like fear or anger.
♦ You feel out of control when you feel full of anxiety from projecting forward into what might happen.
♦ You feel out of control if you feel lost or confused.
♦ You will never feel out of control if you are calm, relaxed and happy.

If you feel out of control, you want to act to make yourself feel safe. You may:

♦ batten down the hatches
♦ organise things
♦ reorganise things.

Anything rather than wait and see what happens, and simply respond to that. Companies are the worst for this. Crisis looms but has not hit and so they reorganise. It is a diversionary tactic, a refusal to look at the real source of the difficulty: we must do something to give an illusion of being in control. This is an example of what we were talking about in the last chapter, creating illusory change.

> We trained very hard, but it seemed that every time we
> were beginning to form up into teams, we would be
> reorganised. I was later to learn in life that we tend to meet
> any situation by reorganising. It can be a wonderful
> method of creating the illusion of progress while creating
> confusion, inefficiency and demoralisation.
> Caius Petronius AD26

Sometimes the response is 'let's do something to the person',
to get them back into control for us so that we feel more
comfortable.

Controlling people

First we want to control people. This can be the worst
demonstration of our unskilful behaviours.

◆ We want people to behave in ways *we think appropriate.*
◆ We want them to think what we think, do what we do, act
   as we act, to like the things that we like.
◆ This makes us feel comfortable because they are our
   mirrors. If they are mirroring back what we want them to it
   feels better, it eases the inner tension we feel with our own
   illusion and separation.

So if they do what we want them to do, they mirror back our
OK-ness and we feel comfortable. But at what cost to the other
person? If they are doing something purely for our sake, what
does that say about us?

Accepting the differences

If we can accept that everyone is different, not wrong or right,
there is no problem. But if we are not very confident about our
individuality, our uniqueness, our right to be exactly who we
are, then we feel threatened. And in feeling threatened we see
'them' as the threat so we seek to control that threat. If we feel
comfortable with our self we do not need to control other
people.

It always comes back to feeling comfortable with yourself,
then you feel comfortable with everything around you. As

without, so within. The reflection in the mirror. So we want other people to behave in a way which we can control. If they do not, we feel angry with them, or disappointed or betrayed by them or we might even manipulate them into doing what we think they should do, using guilt or anger:

◆ if they've got good self-knowledge and esteem, you can't succeed

◆ if they're easily manipulated, you will achieve some success at the expense of honesty.

> Any behaviour or action is dishonest if it is not done from a completely free will.

Controlling situations

The source of most stress is our inability to let things happen and simply respond.

◆ We want the situation to develop as we want it to so that 'if I do that, this will happen next', not 'I do this and see what happens next'.

◆ We've already decided how the situation will develop and then go through the confusion of things not going as expected.

We must recognise that we create all our anger, anxiety and fear when life doesn't work out as we had planned. So the more we want things to be as we think they should be, to control things and people, the less likely we are to get that because we need to learn to let go of those control feelings and wishes and let things be as they will be.

If we want to be more happy, contented and peaceful, we can send that wish out but we cannot choose what that means – having this car, that job, this lover, that amount of money. That will not make us happy.

◆ If we release the desire for happiness and let it come back in the best way possible, we are not putting limits on what we can receive.

◆ If we release the message that we want this car in order to be happy then we might get that car but the happiness could be temporary and therefore illusory.

So we release the 'energy message' of what we want, and allow it to return in the way most appropriate for us to recognise fully *that which we really want*, that deep sense of happiness. When we no longer want to control situations they become fun, like a fairground ride, never knowing quite what is round the next corner but trusting it will be an adventure.

Controlling relationships

We tend to have set ideas of how people should behave in relationships, of what husbands and wives, or sisters or brothers 'should' do. In some ways it is easier to behave according to fixed roles. In the past this is how life was organised – you knew where you stood and just got on with it but at the expense of the individual sense of fulfilment. Now we want a life that reflects ourselves. We don't want a whole chunk of us being ignored or denied, that is not living according to our truth.

> The real meaning of freedom is knowing and living your own truth.

We often expect other people to stick to the roles we have created for them, and to fit in with each other for our convenience. This is how they should be – sisters, children, parents, friends, colleagues, bosses etc. This is the basis of all stereotyping and prejudging.

Case Study _____

David is 16 years old, has long hair and an interest in motorbikes and leather jackets. Everyone who knows him recognises how calm and mature he is for his age, and very gentle. David feels frustrated by reactions from old people walking past him. They almost flee from him on the street because they see his appearance and prejudge his potential intentions. They fear that he might be a mugger because he is a young man in a leather jacket. Their expectations make it highly likely that one day they will be mugged by someone in a leather jacket. Not David of course. They create their reality and it is based on nothing that is real in any other perception. But to them it is real and will become a reality in every sense. _____

This case study illustrates how one group in society is

stereotyped and treated with disrespect by older people who have decided they 'might be bad'. If young people feel disrespected by older people, why should they show them any respect in return? They often do, because sometimes they have more integrity and compassion than their elders as they have less fear.

Creating structures of belief

Not only do we create experiences through our thoughts, we create people too. The person we think exists, never does. We create the image of 'who we think they are' and often 'who we think they ought to be', a basis for judging and failing.

◆ We create a template and impose it on that person.
◆ When they do not meet the image we hold, we get angry and upset with them.
◆ We all do it to each other far more often than we would like to recognise.
◆ We don't like it when it is done to us incongruently with our own self-image.

This final point is the most important one: *we* must stop doing it to others *first.*

Many of our templates are based on images from media influences. One powerful influence comes from love songs. They tell us how you will be treated when you are in love, or what to expect from a lover ... Is that really true? Is that our real experience?

◆ How much are we influenced by these words?
◆ To what extent are we disappointed when they do not develop into our reality?

Try it now

Stand in front of a mirror and sing the words of some love songs to *yourself.* What happens? The words then become true in a far more powerful way:

◆ can't live, if living is without you
◆ you're all I need to get by
◆ if you leave me now, you take away the bigger part of me
◆ all that I have is all that you've given me.

Try it. It works. It is yet another example of the mirroring principle: that what is outside you is a *reflection of what is inside you*.

So if you do not like the outside, look at changing the inside first. *Love yourself* as you want to be loved and then it will happen outside too. These songs become affirmations of what we need to do for ourselves, not what we need from other people. That is the basis of our disappointment with others. We have got to get over the idea of seeing people as 'who we think they should be' in the context of their role in our life and see 'who they really are' within that context. We mustn't impose the relationship role on them, we must allow them to play it as themselves.

Controlling outcomes

We want to control the outcomes of our efforts.

◆ If this happens, that will result.
◆ If I do this, I will get that.

Sometimes you will, because thought creates reality. Sometimes you get your outcome if that is what all of you believes will happen. And sometimes you don't, because if you have any conflicting beliefs which drive it away, then you will get what your thoughts created. But it may not be what you wanted or expected.

> The outcome you get shows you what you really believe, not what you want to believe.

What we really want is mostly to be happy. We think 'this will make us happy', so we put our thoughts on this outcome in the belief that it will. It doesn't happen because happiness does not lie in something or someone out there. So there is a conflict between the human self, the ego, wanting this or that, and the higher self wanting and understanding the truth about happiness and trying to teach us what it really is.

◆ If we don't get what we think we want we get what we need, in order to teach us that this will not bring happiness.
◆ If we do get what we think we want it can also teach us that

this will not bring happiness.

Either way we are being shown that lasting happiness is not to be found outside yourself. It merely reflects what you already have.

Sometimes there are so many layers of want that all we get is confusion, which is the mirror of what we have inside.

Contradicting our own thoughts

If you send out contradictory beliefs, you will not get the outcome you expected. And that is the basis of your disappointment. If your thoughts are clear, the outcome will be better than you hoped for and the more you 'let go' the more this becomes true.

Self-reliance and going with the flow

The basis for wanting to be in control of the things and people out there is our lack of trust that things will work out as we want them to be. But most of all:

◆ We lack the trust in our own ability to deal with that outcome.

◆ We lack trust in our own behaviour and responses.

◆ We lack the trust that we will manage whatever life throws at us.

There is a wise saying from many traditions, *the burden is never greater than you can carry.* That is why we can trust. Usually though we don't feel we can go with the flow, we don't believe we can deal with the unexpected. But when it happens, is it not your experience that you do manage? So it is not even the reality of the unexpected that is the problem, it is the thought of it.

Expectations and perceptions

Because we also tend to judge ourselves:

◆ we judge our ability to cope with the challenge

◆ we judge that we didn't cope as well 'as we should have'.

Instead of learning what to do next time, we chastise ourselves for not knowing before. Yet how could we? We needed that context to understand the lesson. This comes from the fear of being criticised or rejected for doing our best. That is the basis of our fear of the unexpected, and hence our desire to control it.

> What you want to control is your fear of what the outcome actually might be.

It is our attachment and desire to control which is the basis of our pain, not the outcome itself. Most of our pain, either emotional or physical, is to do with our inner conflict and desire to control what is. *Acceptance is the art of non-control.* Pain is mainly the resistance to change – this is what causes the difficulty, not the change itself.

Summary

Acceptance and control are two ends of the same dimension, one based totally in fear and the other in trust and love. We are all somewhere along that dimension and in different places in different aspects of our lives.

- ◆ Acceptance is the art of allowing people and events to develop in their own way.
- ◆ Controlling people to gain the response you desire is always dishonest and a betrayal of both parties.
- ◆ Controlling a situation is the basis of all stress and conflict.
- ◆ Learning to go with the flow, and allowing life to bring adventure towards you, brings the greatest rewards.
- ◆ Accepting that there is no right or wrong and being able to learn from every experience is the only way to find your heart's desire.

To forgive everything, and everyone is the greatest gift you can give yourself.

Forgiveness

F orgiveness is another key principle to living the life you want and finding true happiness. The dictionary definition of forgiveness includes a definition of it as 'to cease to feel anger'. That is quite an enlightened definition, because most of the time we are:

◆ angry with ourselves for making mistakes
◆ angry with other people for not doing what we think they should

and that is basically what we have to forgive.

◆ Whom do we forgive?
◆ What do we forgive them for?
◆ Why do we find it hard to forgive?
◆ Why do we find it harder to forgive some people and easier to forgive others?
◆ Most important of all, what about self-forgiveness?

Why do we find it hard to heal ourselves by forgiving and letting go? If we hold negative, fear-based feelings and beliefs, we are expressing them through our energy field. Like attracts like, so back the uncomfortable experiences come, into our life. You can call this karma, cause and effect, self-fulfilling prophesy, we create our own reality, whichever approach you prefer. It is a principle and applies uniformly across experience.

> Energy principles state that whatever we keep inside is going to be 'out there', and if we release and forgive it disappears from our life.

So why do we find it so hard to forgive? The answer becomes apparent once we explore the nature of forgiving.

The real meaning of forgiveness

Sometimes words have heavy agendas which make it hard to respond to them openly. This creates blocks to our recognition and ability or willingness to work with certain concepts. Forgiveness is often one of these, which is why it can be so hard.

◆ Perhaps we have been made to forgive someone when we were not ready to do so.

◆ We might have been punished and 'forgiven' for doing something we did not believe was wrong in the first place.

◆ Forgiveness has allowed someone to avoid taking responsibility for their actions.

In all three cases the concept of forgiveness has been twisted and manipulated away from its true intention. So we find it hard to respond openly to the word and concept of forgiveness.

> Forgiveness benefits one person – you. Others benefit because you forgive yourself, not them.

If you break the word forgiveness down it becomes *for giving* – being in favour of giving to, for example, yourself. Alternative words include:

◆ **Acceptance**: a kind of pre-forgiveness because it is non-judgemental so there is nothing to forgive. Acceptance suggests that everything is OK, that was a mistake and we accept it, let it pass. It is gone.

◆ **Atonement**: being at one with yourself, an absence of conflict, inner peace.

All the above can only occur when we have released our own aspects of fear, anger, shame, guilt etc.

Watching life flow by

Buddhism teaches that you can watch these experiences, just like sitting on a riverbank watching the river pass you by. It doesn't affect you and doesn't touch you. Then, if you just accept everything, there is no forgiveness needed. So learning forgiveness is a crucial stage in letting go and self-acceptance. The philosopher and teacher, J. Krishnamurti, teaches that we should allow our emotions to exist, to observe them and remain uninvolved, unattached and not deny them. To watch and accept them but not to be driven by them.

Perfection and imperfection

By beginning to forgive the 'out there', we are beginning to accept who we are and our own wonderful imperfections. The word imperfection is based on a judgement that something is not as 'good' as it should be. But again, by whose criteria?

Some of my worst characteristics, according to my teachers and parents as a child, have proved to be my absolute strengths in adulthood. It was just a matter of allowing them time to mature and develop. This is true. All the teachings in this book are the result of changes in the lives of both authors. We know this works.

Often our imperfections are judged to be so because they cause a difficulty for someone else. So it is their opinion that you have an imperfection. This judgement, with some additional fears like rejection, shame, and guilt, make a powerful concoction for self-rejection and denial of our true potential. But if we accept:

◆ all our relationships are really a series of lessons for us to learn from and through
◆ in return we provide learning opportunities for others

then:
◆ we are perfect in our imperfections
◆ our imperfections create the best possible teaching for all people who learn from us
◆ their imperfections are the best ones for us to learn from.

So we are perfect in our imperfections. We are unique. The people in our lives are there particularly to learn what they can from us, and for us to learn from them. We both learn from and teach each other all the time in all our interactions. We are all perfectly equipped to teach and learn what the people around us are there to learn from and to teach us. Then there is nothing to forgive because no one is doing anything to anybody, it is a mutual exchange, it is all a gift. Eventually we do move beyond thinking that there is anything to forgive.

Victimhood

We find forgiveness hard because we can't let go of the idea of our victimhood, that we were hurt by someone else. So what exactly is it that has been hurt, our pride? Usually. Pride is who we want to be, not who we really are. It is a false sense of self-importance rather than the true value of who we are.

◆ Pride is a denial of the beauty and balance of all that we are, and a denial of our growth potential.

◆ Pride is often confused with self-esteem which is an honest appraisal and acceptance of self.

> Nothing happens in our lives that does not reflect something inside us. No one has done anything to us. They just show us our own pain and give us an opportunity to recognise and heal. To forgive. We choose to ignore these opportunities and feel the 'victim'.

Once we forgive, we diminish the ego and allow our loving self to emerge.

Whom do we forgive?

First of all we forgive other people; that is, to cease to feel anger towards them. Let's explore this in depth and recap many other points from earlier in the book.

Other people represent our mirror, they reflect back to us what we most need to know in ourselves. They are the reflection of everything inside us. And we judge them for this as a denial of our own conflict. So what is happening?

Consider this

◆ Have you ever felt the person other people think is you doesn't coincide with the person you feel you are?

◆ Do you believe them and not yourself? Who knows you best? Anyone?

If you asked two people to describe you they would come up with two different people. But to them that is really who they think you are. Can you see the difficulties this creates? However much we think we know another person we never can, because the person is not a fixed reality. Every five minutes we become someone else. It is the ego that 'needs to be a self'. How much do we judge the person we were rather than accept the person we are now?

Buddhism teaches that we don't have a self. Instead we are made up of five aggregates or aspects of experience:

1   the physical or material
2   the sensory, including mind
3   the perceptual
4   mental activity and actions it leads to, called volitional acts
5   consciousness.

Our experiences and interpretations of things that happen within those five areas make and give us a sense of identity, as if we exist.

Try it now   If we are subject to change in these states listed above, then we become different daily. As each of those states moves on through new experiences, it creates a different self.

♦ Are you exactly the same person as last week or do you think there is something different?
♦ How about last year or when you were a teenager?
♦ Make a list of ways in which you have changed over the last two years in each of those five areas listed above.

Now you have a sense of how much you have changed. But other people aren't necessarily aware of those daily subtleties. They have their fixed sense of 'who you are'. A common experience when people change is for others to appear to try to undermine those changes, and make you go back to who *they* think you are. This makes them feel safe and in control of the relationship. They know where they stand with you. This arises because they cannot let go of their image of you and are not prepared to accept the new you. It is to do with power and control.

Hard lessons and horrid mirrors

We think we know other people, and they think they know who we are. But in reality everyone is simply a mirror of things going on inside us. When we forgive them, what we are forgiving them for is for showing us what we most need to know about our self. The hardest aspect of this is forgiving the people who highlight our weakest behaviours, who show us our worst. We blame them for 'making us do this' but really they are just showing us what we need to learn next.

No one ever 'makes' us do anything, we just believe they do. But we believe the person who hurts us the most is bad because of the pain they have inflicted. Their actions might not have been very emotionally aware or skilful, but it was not us they did it to, it was themselves. We just happened to be the convenient person who was able to take on the corresponding role because of what we held inside us. So who do we need to forgive? The other, for acting out their pain and inner turmoil, or us for allowing ourselves to be used?

Case Study _____

Jane's character was strong, determined and independent. She liked to ask questions, challenge assumptions and expose 'meaningless' rules. Her childhood was full of criticism and punishment for 'being a difficult child'. The punishment included physical beatings, constant rejection of her qualities as an individual and being told she was such a bad person that this would make her behave well. At school she underachieved dramatically but still managed to scrape through with some exam qualifications. For this she was punished. She felt a great deal of fear and anger towards her parents and became moody and sulky, arguing a great deal. For this she was punished.

As a young adult she managed to find people who accepted her just enough to feel safe. But she was clingy, self-pitying and even manipulative towards them, to test their loyalty. Unconsciously she felt that they must be lying when they said they liked or loved her because 'she was a difficult person who would be rejected once people found out who she really was'. That was what her parents had told her, and they must be right.

After years of struggling and emotional upheavals, Jane finally accepted counselling and recognised the real truth about her and her parents. She recognised their emotional poverty and childhood pain being repeated in her life. She made dramatic progress in all aspects of her life but found it hard in the end to forgive her mother who did not protect her from the beatings and often caused them by her complaints as soon as her father walked in from work.

Finally Jane realised that it is all right to forgive your mother or father but not to allow them to continue to treat you like this. She kept her mother at arms' length, thus removing her influence. This established her boundaries. Although her mother refused to acknowledge these rules, Jane maintained them in every way she could while she allowed herself to heal through her new experiences which were completely away from the influence of her mother. Finally she was able to include her mother in small areas of her life and forgive herself for having believed her mother's judgements of her. Her mother could no longer affect Jane's life so Jane was no longer afraid of her. This allowed her to feel love and compassion for her mother's suffering and accept that if her mother did not want to change, it was her choice. Jane forgave, accepted and became at one with herself. _____

We can forgive others for being less than wonderful, but we don't like it when other people show us up for being imperfect. It is far easier to be generous out there than when it hits close to home. Jane became the very things her parents told her she was, aggressive and angry, fearful and rejecting. She became like her mother and father, behaving in ways they did. She mirrored their behaviour and they punished her for it. After counselling she no longer behaved in these ways.

◆ We quite often direct anger at people who confront us with something we don't like in ourselves or we don't want to hear about, as an attempt to stop them.

◆ We find it easier to recognise the faults in other people because we believe it is them, not us.

This approach to forgiveness is a form of judgement, and judgement of others is based on how we feel about ourselves.

Forgiveness is not judgement

Forgiving someone else is based on the false premise that you are right and they are wrong, there is something for you to forgive them for because 'they have done something to you'. That is an elevation of the ego self. If someone is violent to you, it is reflecting back your own belief in your victimhood, which attracts that behaviour to you.

> Our anger is our denial that we are what is being shown to us, and that it could be true.

We get angry for being shown what we fear but know to be true. This is an ego defence and a measure of how much our ego is in control of us. The more we react, the more our ego is in control of us instead of us being a master of it. The ego doesn't like to let go of hurt perceptions and forgive. The ego likes to think 'I am the aggrieved party and you are the aggressor', it doesn't like to think 'that is only happening out there because of what is in here'. The ego also prefers conflict because that gives it a sense of power in its own existence.

- It is part of the illusion that the ego has power.
- It is part of our difficulty when we deny our right to be imperfect.
- Our denial of our imperfections and lack of acceptance of ourselves as we are comes from our desire to see ourselves as right or wrong.
- The judgement we make of ourselves is behind all this.

It is our belief in others' judgement of us that creates the anger in us. If we don't believe what they judge us to be we don't react to it, then it's meaningless and we say 'It's their problem not mine', which is as it should be.

Dealing with judgement

If someone says you're stupid sometimes, recognise your choice of responses. Instead of being furious with them for saying that you could reply 'Yes, you are absolutely right, sometimes I can be a complete idiot and sometimes I can be really brilliant and isn't that true of everybody?' You then take the power out of that situation because you have owned it and there is nothing to forgive. You have taken the power back.

The person may be saying this for one of two reasons:

- Just to put you down. If they are doing that you have taken the power back if you own the criticism.

◆ To help: it is a genuine offer of feedback. They are just being honest and helping you to think about the way you come across. It may show you why people respond to you in a certain way that makes you feel unhappy.

Criticism is a chance for you to look at something. That is the gift, even though it may be uncomfortable. If we say 'Yes, I can be daft but so can everyone else, but I can also be excellent', we are keeping the power within us. There is nothing to forgive then, no self-righteousness, nothing to say I am right and you are wrong, I am the victim and you are the aggressor. There is nothing to forgive because we have taken it and owned it for ourselves.

Recognising the belief in two powers

The act of forgiveness is a statement of belief in two powers, in judgement, in right and wrong, good and bad. If I have to forgive you, then you have done something wrong and I am the aggrieved. It is actually confirming our sense of separation from the fact that everything is connected and one. Ultimately we need to let those beliefs go as much as we are able.

Forgiving ourselves

In the last few chapters we saw how most of our anger is based on our need to decide what the outcome should be, or how someone should behave or how they should respond to us. It is our need to control that has made us angry, rather than what that person has done. They have not been the person that we thought they should be. So whom do we have to forgive here? If they have not been the person we thought they should be and we are angry because of it, who has actually made the mistake, who is the person we need to forgive?

It is us. We are the one who created that expectation and we are the one who is responding to having that expectation thwarted. We have to forgive ourselves for having expectations and learn to let go.

> We have to accept that things are the way they are. We have neither the ability nor the right to control, manipulate or decide what should or shouldn't be. We have to learn acceptance.

Forgiveness is:

◆ Taking responsibility back to ourselves for everything that happens to us.
◆ Saying I need to forgive myself for expecting too much of myself.

So we often need to forgive ourselves for:

◆ not being able to know things earlier
◆ not seeing the truth sooner
◆ letting other people have power over us
◆ being human and fallible.

Learning how to manage life and to develop emotionally is like learning to walk for the first time – all the time. As soon as we have mastered one bit there's another skill to learn. We are beating up our own inner toddler, who is still learning to walk, let alone to jump, run, skip and hop. We are being very unfair to ourselves.

Finding forgiveness for all

If we consider our attitudes to other people – because this is part of it even though it comes back to our self – we have to begin by thinking 'I forgive this person'. Why is it easier to forgive some people more than others for being less than perfect? If some people are accepting of us then it is very easy to accept them. Sometimes you mess up with people you are close to and easy with, and sometimes they mess up, but anger is shortlived. There is nothing to forgive because it is just a process of total acceptance, there is no difficulty, no struggle.

Forgiving first

If we forgive some people why can't we do it with others? We find it difficult to forgive the people who do not forgive us, taking it from the mirroring point of view. We have to forgive them first in order for them to forgive us, but that is the harder thing to do.

We don't like somebody, because they are judging us:

◆ They judge us because we find them difficult.
◆ They are showing us things that we don't want to know and we are angry with them. This encompasses all the other reasons why we don't like people.
◆ We use that as a justification for remaining angry with them.

To use the example of parents, we often use their emotional unavailability as a justification for being angry with them for many years. We are completely unable to forgive them for things they have 'done to us'. We are a victim here, until we are able to see that what they taught was brilliant, albeit uncomfortable. Be compassionate to them, they also had difficult childhoods.

Once you start realising that, there is no justification in not forgiving them; they were doing the best they could with what they knew. So we have to say 'You are the way you are because of what happened to you. I don't have to buy into that any more. That is not my problem.'

How do you make that step to forgive someone without suppressing it? It comes back to acknowledging:

◆ What experience of pain and separation was behind their behaviour.
◆ Accepting that they didn't know any better, they did as was done to them.
◆ They were also struggling to find a sense of self, love, value and self-worth.

If they behaved hurtfully then look with compassion at what must be inside someone to make them behave like that. The more unskilfully they behave, the more inner anguish and turmoil they have. Would any of us want to feel that? Everything outside is an expression of what is inside. Would *you* want to live with those feelings all the time? We can recognise that the way someone is behaving is an indication of how much conflict and self-denial they feel inside.

> We can always make the choice not to give that person power in our life any more. That is an expression of love and respect, even towards our mother or father. It is our right and a duty to our self.

Once we learn the lesson and let go of our victim attitude, it is a tremendous gift. You can say 'I am really glad for that experience. I never want to go through that again.' The chances are you will never have to because you don't see yourself as a victim any more. You become the conscious creator of your own reality.

Forgiving the past

As children we often feel powerless, there is less choice in 'allowing it' to happen. But in adulthood we just accept the need to forgive all that happened to us as children and to become at peace, at one, with our self. Forgiving is:

1 Letting go of feelings. If you let go of the pain you are still objectively aware of what has gone on. This is the part that is our learning.

2 Letting go of the intellectual attitude behind it, which is the judgement and justification for remaining angry. This is not a feeling, it is a concept of victimhood that causes feelings.

If we can let go of the concept, the feelings will follow. It happens in the following way:
◆ First an intellectual decision or choice.
◆ Then it becomes emotional, we feel the forgiveness and release the anger and pain.
◆ Then it becomes automatic or organic – that is the way that you are.

That is how we learn; what takes knowledge into true learning. As J. Krishnamurti says, knowledge is meaningless until you feel it also, then it is true learning. Real intelligence comes from experiencing what is, in the present, not thinking, which is based in the past.

Ego tricks and forgiveness

Our ego wants to see things in terms of 'I forgive you, because I am so good and you are so bad, I forgive you for your sins against me.' That means the ego is thinking 'I've got it licked. I can do the forgiveness stuff *and* I can keep control here through guilt manipulations.'

This can apply to ourselves too. You may say I forgive myself for being so stupid, but this is not accepting you are doing the best you can. It is actually saying you *were* stupid, so you are still judging yourself.

The real meaning of forgiveness is to become at one with yourself. The only person you need to forgive is yourself. When you are at peace with yourself you know that nothing was ever, or can ever, be done to you. There is nothing to fear and so you have no fear. That is actually the final stage of atonement, having no fear because there is nothing that can ever or has ever been done to you. If someone makes you feel angry, forgive yourself for allowing it.

◆ If someone makes you feel guilty, forgive yourself for punishing yourself.

◆ Do this not for them but for yourself.

Try it now

Think of all the lessons you have learned from other people – hard, painful lessons.

1 Think what it would be like if you had been your own teacher, trying to get that lesson across when you didn't want to know or hear it. People who were your teachers had to work very hard, they had to put themselves through some amazing stuff in order to get you to learn that lesson. They did it in the best way they could to make you really notice it. Think of how resistant you were as a student. How does this perspective feel now? Do you have a sense of atonement and peace?

2 Think about when you taught someone a hard lesson, how much anguish it put you through at the same time. How much turmoil, struggle and fear did you experience in order to teach that person something they didn't want to learn? You did your best, just as they did theirs.

Healing and forgiveness is a conscious act, a decision. It is an act of love to ourselves and enables abundance to come into our lives. Once we have learned to give to ourselves, we are able to receive the abundance that awaits us.

Summary

The real meaning of forgiveness is not to forget, it is to become comfortable and accept what happened and to have no judgement about it. To be at peace within.

- One of the best ways to have nothing to forgive is to take responsibility and say 'Yes, you may be right, I will think about that, thank you for bringing it to my attention.' You retain your power and integrity, so there is nothing to forgive.

- Forgiving does not mean forgetting, it means accepting the learning from the situation and not holding on to the negative anger. Forget the injustice, or the belief in the injustice, but don't forget the learning.

- Forgetting implies ignoring or even possibly suppressing the memory, which is not a good idea. It will always come up again, one way or another.

- We often don't trust that things will get better if we let negativity go. We think somehow we have lost something that is ourselves, but all we have lost is a sense of victimhood.

- The best reason to forgive and let go is because if you do everything suddenly starts getting much better. The difficult part is to trust that this is the case.

CHAPTER 11

Letting Go

We often hear the term **letting go** when talking about personal or spiritual advancement.

◆ What does it mean?

◆ How can letting go change the way we live our lives?

Letting go does not fall into the same category as an expression such as 'what will be will be'. This is a nebulous catchphrase which avoids the truth behind life's problems. Letting go, on the other hand, if properly understood, means much more. It requires:

◆ taking action

◆ making changes

◆ being accepting in your approach to living

◆ taking nothing personally.

We have responsibility for the shape of our lives, and living does take some effort. To sit back and say 'what will be will be' is not good enough. It is saying 'I won't bother putting any effort into my life, I'll just sit back and hope that everyone else will give me the things I want, and if they don't I will feel sorry for myself and pretend it couldn't have been any different.'

What is letting go?

Letting go is something which many people fear more than anything, which is why we left it until the last chapter to explore in depth. The reason for the fear is that each person is bound up in the pre-set ideas and patterns of their lives and the thought of letting anything go is contrary to the way they see the world. Most people go through life acquiring, whether it is possessions or emotional experience. This acquisitive form of existence is all they know, and in many cases all they want to know, but it carries with it a great burden. *The more you acquire, the more you carry*, and the greater your fear of loss.

Is letting go losing?

◆ Do you really give up anything?

◆ Or do you actually gain by an incredible paradox?

It's rather like the apple, you won't know until you take the first bite. But listening to people who have tasted the apple is a good place to start.

Try it now

Take a look at yourself. How many of the possessions around you are essential to your well-being? Not how many do you covet or desire, but those without which you could not live a satisfying life. We all need warmth, food and shelter, but beyond these three basic needs what else do we possess? The following is a list which you might like to use as a start for your own.

◆ hi-fi

◆ wide-screen TV

◆ dishwasher

◆ new car

◆ microwave

◆ computer

◆ leather sofa.

When you have made your list think of:

1 How much effort has gone into acquiring these things?

2 How you would feel without them? Don't worry if they are important to you, if they weren't you wouldn't have them, would you?

3 Supposing tomorrow something happened and these things no longer existed. How would you feel? Lost? Deprived? Angry? Somehow diminished? If so, what would this say about you?

The implication of the exercise above is that in some way, at some level, these material objects express the way you feel about yourself. As such they actually become the 'person' that you are, for without them you are not the same. You aren't as happy, or perhaps as confident, as you were. We collect some things about us because they:

◆ save us time
◆ make us feel good
◆ give us status.

They are important to the way we are.

What's in my loft?

Now that we've had a brief look at the 'essentials', what's in your loft, or garage or shed? Don't say there isn't anything – everyone who has a loft or garage fills it with those possessions which were once of vital importance. Think of those things and imagine when someone coveted those items. They were all in a shop once, all brand new. Somebody, possibly yourself:

◆ spent money on them
◆ showed them off to friends.

They made you feel good. What happened? Time passed, circumstances changed. Spend a moment thinking about these things, we will come back to them later.

I don't want to give up my car

So why do we have to let things go, and if we do want to how can we do this? Immediately objections arise in our mind:

◆ Why should I let go of my possessions when I have worked hard for them?
◆ They don't do any harm to anyone else.

Let's look at things from a different angle. Suppose we said you can keep everything you have, but at the same time you can let them go. Feel any better about it? Impossible to do? Not really. What we are talking about is your approach to ownership, to acquiring, to basing your life upon possessions. There is nothing wrong with ownership, we all have to live within the current culture, and if the way life is currently lived requires that we own a car, for example, then that is what we need to do. Where things become distorted is when the object becomes more important than its use. When you live for the object and it begins to possess you. Letting go teaches you to:

◆ understand the reason why you have particular things
◆ explore your relationship with the things you possess.

There are two ways to approach ownership:

◆ one is to firmly grip the thing you want
◆ the other is to let it rest in the palm of your hand.

One takes energy and may become painful. You grow anxious that possessions might be lost or damaged. The other allows you to become detached, to live alongside rather than possess things, to value their contribution to your life but to feel no fear about losing them.

◆ How many of the things you noted down earlier rest in your hand?
◆ How many are you gripping?
◆ How many are you working to pay off? This requires energy just as if you had your hand clenched.
◆ How many of them do you worry about?

Take the person who parks their car on the far side of the car park in case it gets scratched. Isn't that a burden? The clenched hand. How many possessions are replaced not because they no longer perform a function, but because they are not the latest style? Does this make sense, doesn't it use unnecessary energy?

I am not my kitchen units

How do you want to be seen by others? If this seems a strange question ask yourself how many of the things you possess reflect back at you because of the way others view them, and how important that is to you. Are you your kitchen units? If you are:

◆ What happens when your kitchen units aren't as good as your neighbours'?
◆ What happens when they are better?

In the former case your neighbour might feel superior, in the latter jealous. Both are ego games. Is this a good way of living? Does it encourage a positive, harmonious approach to life? We must understand this aspect of ownership in order to allow ourselves to let go of the grip.

> When the object becomes more important than its use, we must consider how we stand in relation to it. If it encourages division between you and others, it is not for your benefit.

Do you really want to be seen as an object yourself? He/she

◆ owns this car
◆ owns this house
◆ has the latest TV
◆ wears the most expensive perfume.

Unfortunately we live in a consumer society in which ownership is seen as equally important as how one behaves. In fact it has become the accepted mode of behaviour.

◆ To be admired you must be seen to have acquired.
◆ To be someone worthy of consideration you have to achieve a certain status.

One of the saddest examples we heard of recently was the couple on holiday who said they were disappointed with the sort of people they were having to share their hotel with. When they were around the pool the only way they knew who they should or should not speak to was by looking at the make of watch other people were wearing!

Letting go is perceptual

When we let go, we release the perceived status an object gives us. It is purchased for its use or aesthetic value and not to impress. It is an avoidance of the truth, a sham, which props up an unsatisfactory life.

> If we live for status we will never be happy, for status separates us from others and means that we are unsatisfied with who we really are.

Think about the way in which you view possessions. If you let go of the things you have, are you prepared to accept a change in status? Remember you are looking for your true self and a way of living your life that fulfils all your heart's desire. Can you really do this if you are living the fantasy of being 'someone' because of what you own?

Try it now	Think of the times you have bought something new and shown it to others. Can you remember their reaction? Were they genuinely pleased, or was there a hint of jealousy? Did you get a sense of pride from being able to show them what you had? Why did you show them? Take a moment to reflect.

Ownership vs freedom

We need to consider the *weight* of ownership. Every object you own is a tie. Whether or not you like to admit it, each thing you own takes up space, most objects need to be insured, some need to be maintained. You cannot afford to leave them, but you cannot carry them with you. The more you have, the more you have to care for, to guard, and sometimes to live up to.

What would you take with you to that proverbial desert island? Think hard, are you living to possess, or living as a truly free spirit? Letting go allows you to understand that objects, unless they are viewed correctly, will tie you down and enslave you. Ask yourself how much of a burden the things you possess represent. If they cause you anxiety, make you work harder just to pay for them, or become a status symbol, then they necessarily restrict you and your personal freedom.

Letting go of emotions

Letting go is necessary throughout our lives, and certainly does not only relate to material possessions. As with material things, we have to come to terms with our relationship with our emotions. Some people:

- deny them and avoid talking about them
- suppress them and fear them
- express them without any restraint
- manage them comfortably and take responsibility for them

◆ seek to recreate the ones we like.

Emotions, like material things, can be accumulated, and some people become attached to them. Instead of saying 'what shall be will be', they say 'I can't help what I feel'. What an admission! To say such a thing is to admit:

◆ you have no control
◆ that you must accept the way you behave no matter what
◆ there is no way that you are going to attempt to do anything about it.

Remember what we said about letting go, that it is a positive action. Letting go will allow you to move away from the position where you can't help what you feel, to one where you choose how you feel.

Try it now	Think about something which makes you unhappy. Is it in the present or something which happened in the past? Often it will be something which happened some time ago. Perhaps there are many things which still upset you. Try making a list. To help you here are some examples to which you might relate.

◆ My partner cheated on me.
◆ When we divorced he/she got more than I did.
◆ The way I was treated as a child left me scarred for life.
◆ My business failed and I have never recovered.
◆ My sibling always got more than I did.
◆ My children love their father/mother more than me.

Now ask yourself why you are so unhappy. Some of the following might apply:

◆ anger
◆ guilt
◆ frustration
◆ fear
◆ jealousy
◆ loss.

What do these emotions achieve in relation to the things on your list? How do they change anything? Can they serve any purpose at all?

The important thing is not to deny or avoid your emotions, but to acknowledge them and question if they serve any purpose. Don't try to feel something that you think you ought to feel, acknowledge what you *really* feel.

I can't help the way I feel

Your immediate response might be, 'I know these emotions don't achieve anything but I can't help the way I feel.' A helpless person having pointless emotions, is that how you want to be? We need to understand something fundamental about life and the way energy works. If you accept that we are essentially complex units of energy, then you must accept:

◆ that we can only interact with other energy
◆ that the only form of energy with which we can interact is that coming towards us, ie what we call the future.

The past is the result of this interaction. It no longer has any energy, it is spent, therefore when we try to interact with it we find we cannot achieve anything. No matter how often or how strongly we try to drag the past into the present, to change it, we are unable so to do. What we do is to pull a finished thing into the present like a cat throwing a dead animal into the air to try and make it move. We are stuck. Energy can only change other forms of energy. The thoughts we harbour about the past, the things we keep in the loft or the garage of the mind, have no energy outside our own imaginations. They are imprints of a creature which has passed and gone.

What am I to do about the past?

The only positive thing you can do, the only interaction you can have, is with yourself. You cannot do anything else. And all that you can do is to let go. Imagine that your mind is a river of consciousness. Each unsettled emotional experience is a block to the river, a small dam against which the river of thought presses, and this pressure causes the pain we feel. Just like a bruise it extends, but we keep hitting the place where that bruise has formed, making it feel worse and never allowing it to dissipate. We have to unblock this dam, let the emotion drain away, and we do this by letting go.

In order to let go we have to face ourselves. We cannot avoid the truth, which is that we hold on to the past because it gives us security. Without the past we are afraid of the future. It is part of the framework we build of ourselves, and if we give it up what will we be?

> Ironic as it might seem it is of more comfort to us to cling to pain, to discomfort, to an unhappy past than it is to face the future as someone new.

◆ I need to be the damaged child.
◆ I need to be the wounded party in the breakup of my marriage.
◆ I need to be the loser, otherwise what am I?
◆ I have learnt the script and am too old to learn a new one.
◆ If I let go, if I unblock the dam, what will happen? The river of consciousness will flood and drown me. I cannot bear the thought of letting it all out, of freeing this wild thing.

The truth is, it is an imagined beast. The only energy it has is the energy you give it, the energy you have allowed it to have. Because it is the past it cannot have any energy of its own. The laws of nature do not allow for anything else. 'But I feel such pain!' you may say, and 'if there is pain then there must be something there!'

Perception is pain

How do you feel with a toothache? Do you have to think about the toothache to make the pain come? No you don't, it comes of its own accord. This is not the case with unresolved emotion. You only feel the pain when you choose to think about the issue which is unresolved, or something triggers the mind. And because you have allowed the blockage to remain, it hurts.

I still can't let go

Here are some key thoughts you might like to consider if you feel unable to let go. Try them and see whether they are relevant to you.

- ◆ Face yourself and ask 'why am I holding on to these issues?' Is it because you need to be a victim, or that you are afraid of change?
- ◆ Be realistic. Are you a person who needs to control, and the reason these things hurt so much is because you cannot control them?
- ◆ Do you really want to be free, or is it safer to cling on to the image you have of yourself as a loser? If I remain a loser then I don't have to do anything about my life.
- ◆ Do you prefer living in the past, does the future scare you?
- ◆ Are you someone who needs to get even, to have some sort of revenge before you can release yourself? Revenge can never put right the original injury, only produce another.
- ◆ Know that whatever has happened in the past, good things can only come if there is space for them. If you fill your life with the past then you cannot hope to have a future.
- ◆ Use your mind to imagine that block in consciousness, at the same time thinking of the problem which hurts you. Now imagine you have a spade and the block is made of compacted mud. Get in there and start to dig! Open the channels and allow the consciousness to flow over the past and carry it away. You can do this!
- ◆ Understand that everything changes and sometimes we must let go of people, as well as possessions, and old emotions. It is not wrong to say 'this person is no longer someone to whom I can relate', even if they were a person you once loved, be it a partner or a relation. Do not feel obliged to be with someone who causes you distress or discomfort.

Nothing will change unless you want it to, and you have to positively make yourself let go.

Anticipating outcomes

One of the things we do in life is to make plans. It is normal to look ahead, to think about the future and to have certain expectations. In so doing we anticipate outcomes.

- ◆ I am going to get married and live happily ever after.
- ◆ I am going on holiday to Greece and it will all be wonderful.
- ◆ I am going to a new job which will give me all I have ever wanted.

The difficulty with anticipating an outcome is that it seldom fits our preconceived ideas. More often than not we are then disappointed, for life seldom matches the ideal we have in our minds. Should we think about the future? Should we just accept what comes along and make no plans? In managing everyday life, it is not practical to take such a stance, you have to think of the future. But it is *the way in which you think of it* that is important.

> Letting go enables you to look at the future, and accept that things do not always happen in the way you either expect or want them to.

The same is true of the negative approach to outcomes, ie the person who always expects the worst. If you let go of outcomes then the negative energy put into the future no longer exists. If you are truly able to let go then things will go right, they will work out. So try letting go, what can you lose?

What happens next?

We said at the beginning of the chapter that the paradox of letting go is that you don't actually lose at all, in fact you gain. How does this happen?

Nothing new can come into your life unless you give up the old. It is like the loft and the garage, there comes a point where you have filled every available space, and you can't even get to the useful things because of the overcrowding.

Letting go is not a process of disposal. It is a state of mind by which we rethink our relationship with the material, emotional and spiritual. Some people wrongly assume that letting go leads to selfishness, coldness or disinterest. Nothing could be further from the truth. When letting go becomes a way of life for you, your attitude to all things changes. You no longer fear loss in the same way, because loss comes from the fear of having to give something up. If you have not grasped a thing then you will not find it so difficult to give up. It doesn't mean you don't appreciate the universe around you, you just don't want to own it! This applies equally to material things, emotions and people.

> Letting go teaches us that the less we grip, with a fearful, grasping attitude, the more comes to us. You will find that as you let go, some things will drift away from you like leaves floating on water, but others will actually drift towards you.

It can be likened to our relationship with animals. If you attempt to approach an animal that doesn't know you, particularly a semi-wild one, it will try to run away. If you stand still for long enough, more often than not the creature will be drawn towards you. Such an animal will never approach the child who wants to grip it around the neck, and sometimes we are that child, putting our demands first by trying to grasp some things and pushing away the very things we most want.

Attachment, non-attachment and detachment

It is necessary to emphasise a distinction between attachment, non-attachment and detachment. Letting go should not be confused with disinterest in, or distancing oneself, from life. Non-attachment is not the same as detachment. To be detached implies a level of disinterest, 'I'm not involved with this or that, it doesn't matter to me what happens.' Such an approach does not imply a sense of being at one with life, it says 'I am apart from this, I don't want to think about it.'

Being non-attached on the other hand says, 'I know the options, I see what is happening, I will make as skilful an effort as I can to achieve appropriate actions in my life but I will not cling to outcomes, I will not cling to old emotions, I will not cling to physical property.'

Summary

Letting go is a conscious choice and an active process. Nothing and no one can make it happen for us, only we can do it for ourselves. It is a sign of our own self-respect that we work to achieve this gift to our present and future happiness.

◆ You can dispose of all that old rubbish in the mental loft and the garage!

◆ Through letting go you will find greater flexibility of thought, no longer being tied to old feelings and issues. Your desire to possess changes into an appreciation of the important things in life.

◆ As you let go your relationships become stronger because there is no element of possession in them. You know who really wants to be with you, as opposed to those you are trying to hold on to.

◆ Letting go allows you to face the future without the normal structural demands. We all write the future in our own minds, we all want it to be just as we desire, but when you let go you understand the possibility of accepting whatever comes your way, and living freely.

◆ Letting go helps rid the mind of jealousy, guilt, shame and anger, and allows you to rethink old issues afresh.

Appendix 1
Living with Metaphysics

T he aim of these two appendices is to outline the
principles from two approaches to living: metaphysics
and Buddhism. Whilst there are differences, it is their
similarities which are most apparent. Everything we have said
in this book can be found within the teachings of either
discipline. But the beauty of metaphysics and Buddhism is that
they both teach to not believe and follow this because you are
told to but to find it for yourself and make it your own. So we
urge you to live with these principles and see how you can
make them work for you. You do not need to become a
Buddhist or a metaphysician. Be yourself and find what works
for you.

What is metaphysics?

Metaphysics is a branch of philosophy which explores the
nature of existence. It includes all religions and belief systems
and explores their teachings in order to achieve a balanced
understanding of life, specifically in relation to human
experience and how it works. This is the study of 'spiritual
psychology', a term used by Ernest Holmes in his book *Science
of Mind*. Metaphysics offers a whole life approach which
enables us to develop principles and values that enrich our own
experience and the lives of those around us.

We have laid out these principles as a series of laws which
you can apply to every aspect of your life. All these principles
work without discrimination because they cannot be wrong in
universal terms. A principle always applies equally, regardless of
circumstances, it is non-discriminatory. All that happens in the
universe is of the universe and therefore of itself, it cannot be
wrong. It is just part of the process of continual change and

development. You cannot be in something and not of it. If you are of it, you are part of it. If you are part of a whole then you cannot be wrong. It is like saying your arm is wrong but the rest of you is right.

Principles

Principles do not have favourites. Remember that yellow and blue always make green. The principles of metaphysics follow in the same way. The principles work when they are applied but how we apply them is the only variable of the principle, eg too much blue and too little yellow make a very dark green, the other way round is much lighter. Also, which shades of blue and yellow you start off with will create variation. The variation is only in the application and materials, the principle remains the same. We only know *that it works*, we do not yet know why. Yet we would not say this colour blending is magic, or that we do not believe in it, because we are familiar with it. Once we become familiar with these principles they are as easy to live with.

Metaphysics is the study of spiritual psychological principles of life, a system for living which we already use without knowing what we are doing. This lack of awareness is the cause of fear and a sense of separation from the knowledge. Once we understand and apply the principles we find the experiences of fear in our lives greatly reduced and we begin to experience abundance.

The nature of existence

One of the key principles is that of the nature of existence: what does 'it' exist of and how does it work? We use the term **universal energy**, which we also refer to as either **god** or **energy**, to mean all the same thing. There is scientific research which supports these theories but it is still in the debate stage and may stay there for some time, rather as Einstein's theory of relativity and Galileo's understanding of the solar system both took time to become accepted. (This book does not explore the scientific explanations because it is not necessary to incorporate them into your life. If you want to know more, read the chapter on understanding energy in *Trusting Your Intuition* by Sylvia Clare.)

For now, allow yourself to go with the ideas and remain open to them. Energy or god is the substance of the universe, all that exists and all that is in the universe. To be in something you must be of it also. So we are all also **god energy** expressing itself as us.

Evolution

This is a more or less accepted theory which has much supporting evidence but which is not yet proven. It is important to recognise the difference between a theory and fact. It is a key aspect of the experience of understanding the basis of living metaphysically. Theories need to be experienced as reality for them to become a belief.

It is apparent that humans are evolved. From what and to what we do not know but we are still evolving just as society does. Life is a process of perpetual change at all levels. Even a building, our body, society, everything is in perpetual change. Permanence is an illusion. A house, if not maintained, will deteriorate very quickly, so change occurs. On the other hand, if we complete the necessary maintenance and repair work we carry out change ourselves within the existing structure.

Change is also apparent in our bodies. Our cells completely renew themselves every nine to ten months, we are not the same people we were yesterday because we have had different experiences which bring about subtle changes all the time. It is our flexibility to move with change which brings a sense of comfort or discomfort in life. Metaphysics looks at levels of evolving consciousness.

Human awareness

If humans have evolved, we must have started from something and be going to something. As human life is intelligent we must have evolved from an intelligent source. Humans also have two very clear features – self choice and free will. In order to have self-choice and free will we must be free to discover our own natures, our true natures. We cannot be shown how to

exercise free will other than by our own experience and
recognition. Everything has always existed, all the forces of
nature and energy. For example, electricity existed when
humans lived in caves but it was not until our consciousness
was sufficiently raised that we were able to harness it and utilise
it. The same is true of our nature, of free will and free choice.

Human expressions of God

The human expression of God has three aspects, **mind, body**
and **spirit**. The power of three runs throughout mystical and
religious structures and teachings, as a symbol of the structure
of the universe and energy – how it works. Spirit is the
consciousness that is aware beyond the human dimension.
Therefore we must be aware that we live in a spiritual universe
and that everything is governed by thought. Thought is
activated by emotion. So emotion is the creative energy behind
our potential.

Thought creates reality

This is the first principle which we must recognise and work
with. We must control our thoughts and know what they are at
all times. We must know where our thoughts originate. We
must examine our belief system – that which underpins our
thoughts and subjective perceptual interpretations of reality.

Everybody who thinks is practising metaphysics, but
without knowing what they are doing, and so they have the
idea that life happens to them. This is the mistake. Nothing
happens in our life that is not coming directly from our
spiritual energy. We create all our experiences through our
thoughts.

We are studying **life** and the nature of **law** or the **laws of
nature** and how they affect us. This is not supernatural, other
than it is the laws which go over nature, across all nature and
all that exists responds to these laws.

Whose mind is doing the thinking?

Just as all that exists is of the universe, and all is subject to the
same laws, there can only be one mind. We call this God or

universal mind. Whichever term we use, this is the universal mind of which we are each just a part. The mind is *us* expressing as God. God works through us and through our minds so we are God expressing as our self, the individual. There is only one mind but we see it as two, the conscious and the unconscious. We each have this within us and we each call it our mind, **one mind.** The one mind is infinite in all ways, it is omniscient, omnipresent and omnipotent.

Everyone is the same

We are all spiritual beings, even if we do not know it, just as an ant is an ant even if it is unable to think that it is. The mistake is that we think the human reality is the true reality, yet it is only part of the experience of spiritual reality, which is everything and everywhere. By being spiritual beings we are also all-powerful, we have all the power of the universe within us.

> There is one **mental law** in the universe and, where we use it, it becomes our law because we have individualised it.

The mental law is that whatever you think creates reality. Behind the individual mind there is the power of the universe, which has no limits. So the limits you have in your life are those you place there yourself. There is only one mind but we have individualised our part of that mind, rather like rooms in a house or pages in a book. Each one is different, yet cannot exist alone and is part of the whole. Everything in the universe is the same.

All thought is creative, one thought is not more creative than another thought, they all carry equal power. So we must know all our thoughts, including the deeper ones at belief level, or assumption or unconscious level.

Absolute intelligence

Metaphysics accepts an **absolute intelligence** because there is nothing but confirmatory evidence of it in all that exists. Wherever we look we can see it at work, in every atom of everything that exists. We are conscious and we are only a part of the whole universe so we are also demonstrations of the intelligence at our level. Everything is expressing this intelligence at different levels, but everything is part of the whole so not more or less intelligent, just different in what it needs to express. We cannot deny absolute intelligence and consciousness unless we deny we are also conscious. We cannot be in something and not of it. We cannot be a part of something and remain separate. We can believe we are separate but cannot be so in reality. Creation, using thought as the tool of creation, means giving form to this substance of intelligence. Often called energy, or God energy, this substance is all that there is:

◆ it cannot be destroyed or created
◆ it can only manifest itself infinitely as itself which is infinite
◆ it can only change into itself in its limitless forms
◆ therefore it is subject to endless, permanent and continuous change but of itself it is changeless.

These are all aspects of this one law, the **law of mind**. However, to make it simpler to understand with our limited human consciousness, there are divisions to this one law.

Law of mental equivalents

We have to have a thing in our mind, in our imagination, for it to become manifest in our experience. What we imagine becomes possible in reality, but what we do not imagine we cannot manifest. The imagination is the most powerful tool we have as humans because it is the starting point for all that exists and all human development. Tools for this include:

◆ mind maps
◆ collages
◆ visualisations
◆ dreams and prayers
◆ flights of fantasy
◆ beliefs and assumptions
◆ collective unconscious mind of humanity
◆ meditations and trance states.

If we do not:

- believe we deserve something, we will not manifest it
- believe it is possible, it is not
- imagine something, it cannot exist for us
- keep an open mind to all possibilities, we are not open to receive our abundance
- believe we can receive anything, we cannot
- stop insisting on seeing the illusions of permanence and finiteness we separate ourselves from the universe and its potential
- see the good in all that happens to us we cannot experience the good in all.

Opposing thoughts negate each other. Pure thought creates pure outcome – sometimes called the **law of correspondents** – what manifests corresponds with what we think/create using mind.

The law of tendency

What we expect tends to happen. If we expect the worst – bingo. Pessimism, realism and caution create the basis for negative thoughts. Trust is the only mindset that is purely positive. Hope suggests it might not happen, or to someone else not me. Trust that it will happen in the best way for my own good is the only thought that can guide you, whatever happens. The experience is irrelevant, the gift you receive from it in terms of insight and experience itself are the positive outcomes, however hard the experience is to the human aspect of self.

Law of cause and effect

The cause is mind, our mind working within universal mind. Material manifestation is the body of spirit – the body is the effect. The material world is energy expressed as matter. The **law of cause and effect** is also known as **karma**, meaning cause and effect. This is also the basis for the Sermon on the Mount.

> *Judge not that ye be not judged, for with what judgment ye judge, ye shall be judged and with what measure ye mete, it shall be measured to you again.*

What we express is what we send out in energy from us, and this comes back in manifest form. This includes:

◆ what we think about other people
◆ what we imagine is possible or not possible
◆ what we accept from social beliefs
◆ what we desire or long for or dream about
◆ what we fear, feel angry about, reject and judge
◆ what we intend behind all our actions, consciously or unconsciously.

The law of attraction

If we really consider the full implications of thought creates reality we realise that everything in life results from our thoughts. Our thought makes our experiences. The energy we create through our thoughts creates the force of **attraction**. Everyone automatically attracts to themselves just what they are. And wherever we are, however intolerable the situation, we are just where we belong.

This principle, the **law of attraction**, is the basis of evolution and development. We attract to us what reflects what is already within us. We continue to attract similar experiences until we recognise our role in them and learn to change the patterns in our life. The lessons simply get bigger and bigger each time they present to us until we are fully awake to them and start to heal ourselves. Nothing and no one can do anything for us. Everything and everyone can show us that which we need to see in order to recognise our truth and move on from it.

Each person emanates a different vibration of energy which attracts similar vibrations and repels conflicting. It is rather like magnetism, which is a powerful force of attraction to materials that respond to its power yet it leaves other materials unmoved. We use positive and negative emotions in this way, not as opposite ends of an energy form like north and south poles, but as subjective labels of the experience which is of itself neutral.

Although it may seem that we are contradicting the laws of science we are not at all. We confirm that emotional energy and the energies of the aura work according to the same laws. So if we have hostile, fear-based emotional energy in us we attract similar energies and repel positive ones. Likewise with loving based emotions. Our individual emotional core is the nucleus. Nothing can prevent you or make you attract that which reflects your inner energy frequency. The only way to change your life is to change that inner frequency into a loving one.

Law of abundance

The **law of abundance** holds that we can bring into being anything we want in our lives by thinking of it and knowing all our thoughts will create the same manifestation of energy. This is not materialism, this is knowing what we are truly worth and wanting that to reflect in our lives as a demonstration of the abundance of the universe. This includes love and friendship, health, a sense of fulfilment and achievement – all aspects of abundance in life, not just material.

Knowing your true worth means valuing yourself in all aspects of your life:

◆ loving and respecting your body as it is now
◆ acknowledging your needs not your greeds
◆ wanting only that which contributes to your well-being and enables you to give more in return
◆ treating yourself as you would treat others
◆ acknowledging the truth and recognising the illusions, however hard that seems at times
◆ 'seeing' hidden agendas – your own and other people's.

The law of averages

As with all laws the **law of averages** is also impersonal, it does not have favourites or single people/animals/plants out. Abundance is diverse enough for destruction and creation to occur continuously. The goal is increased levels of consciousness for the human expression of spirit, therefore room is left for loss, and trial and error. Destruction is part of the demonstration of law. It shows us the choices we have in life. If the individual expresses their wish to flow with the principles of nature or the law, they move with it and are carried by it, but if they oppose the law they will experience the consequences of the conflict. There is no punishment from god, it is merely the mental equivalent working in accordance with our use of mind. The punishment is only self-punishment until we 'see and work with truth'. It is a freewill universe and offers us a choice we all have to make and recognise. Once we work with truth we are no longer subject to race beliefs, and cause and effect of humanity, but move closer to abundance direct from universal substance.

The law of grace

The **law of grace** moves us beyond human consciousness and allows us to reach our own spiritual truth and awareness. It is similar to teachings of Zen and other mystical traditions. It is where we move to once we recognise cause and effect and can retrain our minds to see only what is. Grace dispels all fears and separation beliefs, and manifests complete 'oneness'. It is not a pardoning law or forgiveness. It can only come from our own consciousness being opened sufficiently.

In the law of grace nothing is impossible because there is no awareness of limitation and no desire for what we do not have. The recognition is we have all we need to achieve greater awareness at all times. It is love in its purest form, that recognises that there are no mistakes – there are only lessons to learn and there is no such thing as evil, bad or wrong. There is only a belief in these things through the belief in separation from the universe.

Dimensions do not exist in a whole, they are constructs applied by human minds. The law of grace exists for us all at all moments, we only have to recognise it and release our lack of trust in the abundance of love available. Love expresses through all that we have or experience.

When these laws are consciously applied, life changes dramatically and throughout this book we have sought to enable their application to real experience.

Appendix 2
The Buddhist Recipe for Living

There are four **Noble Truths** in Buddhism, which relate to *dukkha*, the concept of unhappiness or being ill at ease in our lives. *Dukkha* really relates to all human beliefs in separation, all human experiences of impermanence, including unhappiness because it is not permanent and we can become unhappy if we are happy. The aim is to reach a state of perfect equilibrium, no change of emotions other than a complete state of balanced joy.

The first Noble Truth

Life is *dukkha*, which is suffering. This includes all aspects of human experience, specifically its imperfections and sorrows, frustrations and causes of fear. Buddhism teaches that we must understand the nature of *dukkha*, – exactly what it is, what it feels like – to know it as an experience in all its aspects. Happiness is also *dukkha* because we seek to hold on to it and thus create pain.

The second Noble Truth

The origin of *dukkha*, to understand the nature of desire and attachment, what it is in ourselves which gives rise to these feelings and experiences of imperfection. This is a challenge because it requires us to become objective about all our experiences. Through this we can then move on.

The third Noble Truth

This is the **ending of** *dukkha*, that we must completely rid ourselves of all these experiences and this includes coming to terms with our feelings. Suppressed feelings are still there and must be released.

The fourth Noble Truth

This is the path which will lead to a state of pure bliss, or *nirvana*. Buddhism teaches that we must both know it and stick to it as much as we are able with what we know.

In order to develop these truths in ourselves we must work to increase both our wisdom and our compassion, ie our intellectual understanding and our emotional experience of these truths. We cannot be completely wise whatever we know without compassion, and we cannot be truly emotionally aware without wisdom, they are completely interdependent and of equal importance.

The eight-fold pathway

The **eight paths** are:
◆ Right understanding
◆ Right thought
◆ Right speech
◆ Right action
◆ Right livelihood
◆ Right effort
◆ Right mindfulness
◆ Right concentration.

The eight-fold pathway includes three sub-divisions:
◆ **ethical conduct**
◆ **mental discipline**
◆ **wisdom.**

Ethical conduct

Ethical conduct includes:
◆ **Right speech** – no lies, slander, back-biting, rudeness, impoliteness, abusive language, idle chatter, malicious or foolish gossip.

This means that we will always be courteous and gentle to others in our words to them. We can also choose silence but not when that silence is also a lie. We are allowed to give people honest and non-critical feedback about their behaviour and how it seems to us, to suggest ways they might want to understand themselves better. This is never a justification or abdication of responsibility. We must also respect their right to ignore our comments and must never judge.

♦ **Right action** – moral and honourable behaviour at all times, never acting in a way that you would be ashamed of later or acting dishonestly, eg stealing, intentionally destructive behaviour, any unkind action and any inappropriate sexual behaviour.

Buddhism is open about any sexual act between two consenting people and where no one will be hurt. It does not speak against homosexuality or multiple partners, only that you do what is open and honest to your own truth. It does not promote monogamy or marriage, or celibacy except for priests.

♦ **Right livelihood** – earning your living in a way which does not harm others or the home environment, which really means the whole of the planet.

This especially includes nothing to do with arms and weapons, alcohol, killing or harming animals and cheating others. It also points out that no one livelihood is more virtuous than another and that in today's terms to be a toilet cleaner is equal to being a managing director; which do you miss first if they are not at work?

Ethical conduct is aimed at promoting a harmonious life for both the individual and for others around them, creating a gentle and peaceful society for all. It is also the foundation for all spiritual development and attainment of enlightenment.

Mental discipline

Mental discipline includes:

♦ **Right effort** – the effort required to prevent unwholesome states of mind arising in us, monitoring our thoughts and correcting critical or judgmental thoughts as they start to form, also releasing attitudes of this nature we have developed beforehand.

Then we must intentionally develop compassionate ways of

seeing everyone, of accepting that everyone is doing the best they can with what they know and can do no more according to their consciousness – to acknowledge the toddler in all of us. Finally to continue to develop positive and loving thoughts at all times, which will generate a harmonious energy field around us and benefit all who come into contact with us.

- ◆ **Right mindfulness** – a form of continuous meditative awareness of all our experiences in the present.

How does your body feel, what is it telling you? The body will often tell us what is wrong with our minds and spirit too and we ignore its messages if we do not pay attention to our body. This includes *all* sensory feelings and an awareness of all the activities of our mind too, including both how and when they appear and disappear, especially the ability to notice our automatic thought trains and to detach from them if we cannot quieten them. It means to listen to all the experiences of the moment at all times, to be present and very much in the now. Breathing exercises are a very good method of encouraging a state of mindfulness in ourselves.

- ◆ **Right concentration** – concentrating on feelings of happiness and joy and discarding all forms of desire, worry and fear.

Once we have managed to maintain this we then begin to suppress all intellectual thoughts and to allow our consciousness to focus on tranquility and the **oneness**. We then move on to releasing all active joy and allow happiness to develop into an ability to retain complete balance and harmony of mind. Finally all sensations, even happiness, leave us and we are left with only our conscious awareness remaining. This is called *samadhi*, a state of being perfectly at rest, without any desire to move in any direction at all. From this arises awareness of complete emptiness, a realisation of the complete and ultimate nature of reality – that I know nothing, there is nothing except a state of pure existence.

Wisdom

The final two paths come from wisdom and constitute:

◆ **Right thought** – especially thoughts of love and compassion to all others regardless of how they appear to us.

Love, selfless detachment and non-violence are seen as wisdom, which suggests that people who do engage in these activities lack the understanding of what they are doing and therefore also deserve compassion. They, like us, are doing the best they can and have reached their own level of skilfulness. There is no right or wrong, and releasing thoughts of judgement and condemnation is essential to developing love and compassion in ourselves. It is the desire to judge others which creates *dukkha* in us, not the 'bad behaviour' of others. It is also about making choices which are for our own benefit, like knowing something is bad for you but doing it or knowing something is good for you and not doing it.

◆ **Right understanding** – is understanding the truth about reality, that everything is an illusion created by our own minds.

The real truth is that we are all part of the oneness and cannot be separate from that or from anything around us in the entire universe. Accumulated knowledge is the human form of this reality, but the **ultimate reality** is to see things without names and labels, without words. Words carry with them a series of characteristics and assumptions and concepts, which we must lose because they are human constructs and are not a part of the ultimate reality. This penetration is only possible when the mind is freed from all impurities through wisdom and meditation.

It is the intention that we should seek to develop all eight of these pathways simultaneously, and that they all complement each other. It requires a great deal of self-discipline, self-development and self-purification or forgiveness. It is basically a recipe for living. It is up to each individual to find their own way through these paths, and to honour and respect the right of all others to find their own ways too. We all make mistakes and lose our way, it is unskilful of us to judge that difficulty in others, and compassionate to offer help and support to retrace the path and find the more skilful one.

Buddhism teaches that there is no right way of reaching this consciousness, but that ultimately we all will. The ultimate aim is complete freedom, creativity and peace. It is the intention to find the endless and everlasting qualities of existence, which go beyond the individual nature of humanhood, ie the ego. It is the thought of a 'self' which creates feelings of unhappiness and concepts of attachment: me, mine, etc, also all feelings of fear and the concept of needing protection and a protector or god who is selective.

Self-protection and self-preservation become outmoded feelings if we are endless and everlasting in some aspects of our consciousness. And from what should we need protection if we are all in and therefore of the universe, the oneness. Do we need protection from ourselves only? Ideas of god as a being outside of ourselves, and of our soul as separate from ourselves are part of the cause of all suffering. This goes deeply against the feelings of the ego or the human self and it is this side of our human nature that we overcome as we follow the pathway.

Useful Addresses

If you would like to know more about the ideas in this book, please contact Sylvia Clare and David Hughes about workshops, residential meditation workshops, tapes covering teachings and healing meditations.
PO Box 29
Ventnor
Isle of Wight PO38 3PS

or visit our web site on http://www.btinternet.com/~sylvia.clare/
email: sylvia.clare@btinternet.com

Other sources of information include:
Christine King
Metaphysical Society for the Expansion of Consciousness
PO Box 89
London SE3 7JN

Lynne Beale
The Centre for Studies in Metaphysical Truth
21 Albert Road
London SE9 4SW
Tel: (020) 8402 8948

Further Reading

Stepping Into the Magic, Gill Edwards (Piatkus).

To Have or To Be, Erich Fromm.

Why Me? Why This? Why Now?, Robin Norwood.

Life Patterns, Soul Lessons and Forgiveness, Henry Leo Bolduc (Adventures Into Time Publications)

Creative Visualisation, Shakti Gawain (New World Library).

You Can Heal Your Life, Louise Hay (Hay House Publishing).

Love is Letting go of Fear, Jerry Jampolsky (Celestial Arts, California).

Trusting Your Intuition, Sylvia Clare (How To Books).

Total Freedom, J. Krishnamurti (Harper Collins).

Emotional Intelligence, Danel Goleman (Bloomsbury Press).

What the Buddha Taught, Walpola Rahula (Oneworld).

Mapping the Mind, Rita Carter (Seven Dials).

The Tibetan Book of Living and Dying, Sogyal Rinpoche (Rider Books).